LEADERSHIP IN THE CHURCH:
IN THE EYE OF THE STORM

BY

STAN E. DEKOVEN, PH.D.

LEADERSHIP IN THE CHURCH: IN THE EYE OF THE STORM

© COPYRIGHT 1995 STAN E. DEKOVEN, PH.D.
ISBN: 978-1-61529-016-1

Second Edition October 2010

All rights in this book are reserved worldwide. No part of this book may be reproduced in any manner whatsoever without the written permission of the author except brief quotations embodied in critical articles or reviews.

FOR INFORMATION ON REORDERING PLEASE CONTACT:

VISION PUBLISHING
(760) 789-4700 or 1-800-9-VISION
WWW.VISIONPUBLISHINGSERVICES.COM
PRINTED IN THE UNITED STATES OF AMERICA

Forward

Much of what is taught regarding the ministry is based on the teachings of the church. Throughout the history of the church, the concepts of what a pastor was have changed with the changing perceptions of what the Bible intended a pastor to be. As a student of biblical history attempts to understand the responsibilities and calling of the various ministries mentioned in the Bible, he soon discovers that those understandings change with each new church era.

Much of the problems of the church in modern times can be related to the misunderstandings of the calling, responsibilities, accountability, etc. of each ministry as mentioned in the Bible.

It is understandable that if the church (the Body of Christ) cannot understand the theology of God concerning leadership in the church, the church is doomed to suffer in its efforts to function according to the will and purpose of God.

Strictly speaking, theology is that which is thought and said concerning God. True theology is thus given by the Bible itself as the revelation of God in human terms. But the Bible gives rise to exposition, reflection and presentation. Hence, there is a theology of the church as well as the Bible, though not in addition or opposition to it. It is this theology that we must accept in the effort to understand the "theology of leadership" or as the term is sometimes used, "pastoral theology."

The author has chosen to use the subtitle, "In the Eye of the Storm" for this text on Christian leadership. It is known that within the church there are many storms raging. The storms facing leadership occurr at all times. The minister who accepts the call of God must be thoroughly trained in the theology of his or her particular calling in order to be able to weather the storms of live that are constantly battering against the efforts of the Christian Church. The eye of the storm is that central core around which the storm rages. In the core (the eye) of the storm there is peace and tranquility. The minister, whatever his/her calling, can find this place of peace in the eye of the storm as he/she seeks to become thoroughly aware of his/her calling and embraces the responsibilities of that calling according to the will of God.

LEADERSHIP, GROWTH AND ACTIVATION

One key principle I have learned since the first edition is the importance of activation. Many leaders have stagnated in their ministries; many have quit altogether. One continuous word heard is how difficult it is to lead with the resistant people and difficult circumstances I am in. Well, truly every field is tough, and spiritual leadership is a difficult task. However, it is God's intention to see our ministries successful and our lives fulfilled. I hope the principles provided here will help strengthen the leader in his/her journey. Further, I have become convinced that a primary cause of leadership stagnation is a lack of healthy activation. In Ezekiel 34:16, God's word states the message presented here in beautiful summation are the key elements of ministry leaders must re-focus on. First, we must seek the lost…the great commission motivated by the Great Commandment must be our first passion. Following a close second is to bring back the hundreds and thousands of formerly churched into the fold. We are missing a huge resource for expanding God's Kingdom through the many disgruntled and disenfranchised Christians needing a leader to care. Third, we must re-double our efforts in helping the broken, and strengthening the sick in our ministries.

ACKNOWLEDGMENTS

I humbly acknowledge the tremendous effort put into the development of this original teaching material. I first give the highest praise, honor, and glory to the Lord Jesus Christ. May He reign supreme in our hearts, and come quickly.

Specifically, I would like to thank Dr. Bill Whitlow for having compiled much of the original teaching material, which has been used as a basis for this book. Further, I acknowledge Dr. R. Bryant Mitchell for portions of the "Pastor In His Role" section which has been included in this manuscript.

I also thank the following pastors who have had an impact upon my life and ministry: Rev. Lee Speakman, Dr. Joseph Bohac, Rev. Tim Hicke, Rev. Ted Bonk, Rev. Al Furey, Dr. Ken Chant, Dr. Randy Gurley, Dr. Greg Wark, and Pastor George Runyan. Each has, in his own unique way, contributed to my perceptions and function as a spiritual leader in the Body of Christ. Through their examples, I have learned much about the role and function of pastors (leaders) in ministry.

Further, my appreciation for the love and support of the staff and faculty of Vision International University is immense. Their patience and assistance with this project made it possible.

Finally, to my family, my daughters Rebecca and Rachel, I give my love and gratitude. They, along with their mom, now in heaven, Karen, have endured with me through the trials and joys of leadership in ministry, and still love God, His people and me.

Table Of Contents

FORWARD 3
ACKNOWLEDMENTS 5
FORWARD TO SECOND EDITION 9
INTRODUCTION: THE CALLED ONES 11
SECTION I: THE LEADER IN RELATIONSHIP 15
CHAPTER 1 THE LEADER AND HIS GOD 17
CHAPTER 2 THE LEADER AND HIMSELF 27
CHAPTER 3 THE LEADER AND HIS FAMILY 35
CHAPTER 4 THE LEADER AND HIS CHURCH 45
CHAPTER 5 THE LEADER AND HIS PULPIT 55
CHAPTER 6 THE LEADER AND HIS FRIENDS 63
CHAPTER 7 THE LEADER AND HIS TIME 67
SECTION II: THE PASTOR IN LEADERSHIP 75
CHAPTER 8 THE PASTOR AS FATHER/SERVANT-LEADER 77
CHAPTER 9 THE LEADER AS ADMINISTRATOR 89
CHAPTER 10 THE LEADER AND PROGRAMS 103
CHAPTER 11 THE LEADER IN PUBLIC LIFE 113
CHAPTER 12 THE LEADER, PASTORAL CARE AND COUNSELING 121
CHAPTER 13 THE PASTORAL PITFALLS 137
CHAPTER 14 THE LEADER AND HIS PASSION 147
BIBLIOGRAPHY 153
APPENDIX 155

FORWARD TO SECOND EDITION

Since the first publication of this book I have had the privilege of teaching this topic to leaders around the world. The feedback from students and other leaders has been generally positive, for which I am grateful and gratified. The prompting for doing a re-edit with some additional material was stirred by leaders wanting new insights gained from my continued teaching and leadership experience that was not contained in the first volume.

Introduction
The Called Ones

I was once asked by a zealous Bible student, "How did you know that you were called of God?" After my initial internal retort ("Insolent young man!"), I answered the only way I could. "I just knew."

During a Christian summer camp the same year I was born again, I felt the Lord's "call" into full-time ministry. I was twelve years old. Though many years ago, that day remains fresh and precious in my memory. Most of you who read this book and/or complete the course that accompanies the text, will recall similar times when Jesus warmed your hearts and pressed upon your spirit to serve Him with all your heart.

The sureness of your call must be without question, and tested through life experience. Your certainty must be absolute if you will fulfill your ministry as a spiritual leader.

Once assured of your call, preparation for the task should follow. I say "should," because many a man or woman of God began Christian ministry without the assurance of training, which can, and often does lead to tragic results.

Finally, as you begin your shepherding ministry, the task of being a pastor or faithfully serving in another Five-Fold Ministry gifted office can be daunting. As in most endeavors in life, you will begin with great enthusiasm, zeal and anticipation. Truly, the ministry of the preaching of the Gospel of Christ is the most exciting adventure ever designed by God. But it is not for the faint of heart or weak of stomach. The responsibilities and challenges can be burdensome at best.

For example, the responsibility of administration can be overwhelming, the counseling load seemingly endless. By God's grace, power, and anointing, we can all fulfill His specific mandate upon our life. This book, written, to shepherds (or "becoming-ones") from a shepherd's viewpoint, will hopefully help you avoid some of the problems and pitfalls of leadership in ministry and prepare you more fully for the great task at hand.

WHAT TO EXPECT

In this book, the reader will first encounter the primary relationships and functions that are inherent in ministry, and especially pastoral ministry. They will include:

- The Leader and his God
- The Leader and himself
- The Leader and his family
- The Leader and his church
- The Leader and his pulpit
- The Leader and his friends
- The Leader and his time

The second section of this book will survey in greater detail the role and function of spiritual leadership, and review some of the "nuts and bolts" of active ministry. Included in this section are:

The Leader as father or servant-leader
The Leader as administrator
The Leader and his programs
The Leader in public life
The Leader as counselor or caregiver
The Leader and pastoral pitfalls
The Leader and his passion.

It is my hope as a writer, leader and educator, to present this material in such a way that it will be both inspirational, as well as guide the leader into a greater revelation of his or her role in the Body of Christ. One of the cries of the Church in the 21st Century is to see true leaders emerge who will have the heart of God and an understanding of what it means to be a true servant-leader. The church needs leaders who will shepherd the people of God into a greater knowledge and understanding of the Lord Jesus Christ. I trust that God will bless you as you continue in your journey as a leader in the House of God.

SECTION I:
THE LEADER IN RELATIONSHIP

Chapter 1
The Leader And His God

The leader, or for that matter, any Christian leader, must have a true passion for God. Over the years, many men and women having a sincere and true call of God upon their lives have missed their destiny in the Lord. Their focus was wrong or inadequate. To fulfill his destiny in the Lord, a pastor or any other minister must be able to keep each aspect of the ministerial role in proper perspective; their calling, preparation, intellectual life, and their own personal needs.

Probably the most important focus, and the first with which we must deal, is the Christian leader's focus on his relationship with Almighty God.

Our focus should first of all remain on our high calling. As men or women of God, we have become representatives of God to man.

"Therefore we are ambassadors for Christ, as though God were intreating through us; we beg you on behalf of Christ, be reconciled to God,"
(II Corinthians 5:20 NASB).

The calling of *all* Christians is one of being ambassadors for Christ. But this is especially true for those who are ministers of the Gospel. We have a special, fiduciary responsibility to present God to mankind. This is the great purpose for which Christ came into the world, that he might save men's souls and provide for them entrance into the Kingdom of God.

Secondly, in I Cor. 4:1 the Bible says that we are stewards of the mysteries of God. God has given to ministers of the Gospel the mysteries of the Kingdom. As ministers, we are stewards, we are overseers to assure that the Gospel of Jesus Christ is proclaimed with clarity, power, and purity. This is part of the overall function of the man or woman of God, especially as we recognize our responsibility before the Lord.

Further, Five-Fold ministers are God's representatives on earth. We are to be true ministers, gifts from God to a very needy human race. Through your heart, as a leader, God's love is to be manifest, His goodness shown, and His work demonstrated, often largely through your hands. The message of the truth, the gospel of Jesus Christ, is to be proclaimed through your lips with boldness and without shame.

Thus, your high calling states that you are truly "called," not hired.

> *"No man takes this honor unto himself, but he that is called of God,"*
> **(Heb. 5:4 KJV).**

A true minister of the Gospel will never be "hired" just to please people. He is called to please God. He has a higher form of priesthood even than that of being a servant to the people. First and foremost, he is a servant of God.

The high calling also indicates that the leader is to function as a prophet. The orientation in ministry is a prophetic one. The words of a man of God should echo the very words of heaven. That is, the Lord will speak through you. He is, as it were, a "forth-teller." In himself the messenger is unimportant. It is his message that carries weight; he is to be a voice, a loud-speaker for heaven's divine broadcast.

Many have confused the gift of prophesy, not realizing that when we speak the truth of God's Word, we also speak prophetically of God's plans, purposes, and desires. As we speak forth God's heart under the anointing of the Holy Spirit, that is as prophetic as many of the "Thus saith the Lords" that we hear from congregation or pulpit.

Also of great importance to a leader as a part of this high calling, is the calling to be a shepherd. First Peter 5:2 directs us to feed the flock of God. The Hebrew word for shepherd is *raah*. The Greek word is *poimen*, meaning one who tends a flock, and is the same word as that for a pastor. A Pastor needs to be tender and loving, a guide; in the same manner as is our chief shepherd, the Lord Jesus Christ. Thus, the spiritual leader is responsible before God for all the sheep. He is to be a leader, of course, and not a driver, willing to lay down his life for the sake of the sheep. This takes great patience, especially in light of the many increasing, often inappropriate demands that are placed on the local leader in our modern society. This will be discussed in greater detail later in this volume.

As a leader we are to be an example to all the believers.

"In speech, conduct, love, faith and purity, show yourself an example of those who believe,"
(I Timothy 4:12 NASB).

Everyone involved in ministry knows well that their lives are under a microscope. We are to be a pattern of what God can do with a simple man or woman. He can change and transform us, fill us with His Holy Spirit, and empower us to do things far beyond our natural ability. To shepherd the flock of God is an awesome responsibility, which we do not have the power to do in our own strength. But with the power of the Holy Spirit we can do all things through Christ, who does strengthen us (Phil. 4:13).

A spiritual leader, must be a servant-leader.

"Ourselves your servants for Jesus' sake,"
(II Cor. 4:5 KJV).

Paul the Apostle, though an obvious leader, included himself as a servant. He was a servant in the house of God, and he readily gave of himself for the needs of God's people. Each Christian minister, even as Jesus was a servant, needs to be a servant to the people of God. We must show meekness as Moses did, and as Christ did in his life on earth. Meekness is not weakness, but quiet strength; a willingness to humble oneself, and with the quiet strength of the Holy Spirit, go about doing one's business with gladness of heart. Although Jesus instructs His servants to allow for time of rest, as servants, our working hours are twenty-four hours a day, seven days a week. Later we will talk about some of the burdens of being a servant, and ways to alleviate them. It *is* essential that we have a balanced life in terms of our ministry. We must be concerned about the needs of our family, about our financial security, and other responsibilities important to face. Yet first and foremost, we are servants of the Lord, and then of the people to which He has called us.

Finally, we are ministers. But what does this mean?

"Men shall call you the ministers of our God," (Isa. 61:6 KJV).

First we must acknowledge that all of God's men and women, born again and filled with His Spirit, are ministers of the Gospel of Jesus Christ. Yet, there are ministers, and...there are ministers. The ministers who have higher position or higher calling, in terms of responsibility and authority, are the focus of this volume. God expects leaders to live a life of holiness before the Lord, giving themselves willingly to the needs of others. A Christian leaders life and service is ministry, not just a career. As such, the work accomplished is for a reward, a crown of life, which will ultimately be placed at the feet of Jesus. The highest good or acknowledgment of accomplishment and worth is not to see ones name flashed in neon lights, but to please the heart of our Master.

Because the leaders high calling brings them into relationship with God and His people, preparation for the ministry to which one is called is essential. To introduce this very important topic, there are three important areas of life we must focus on, as preparation for ministry begins.

GOD AND THE SPIRITUAL LIFE

"Who has saved us, and called us with a holy calling, not according to our works, but according to His own purpose and grace, which was granted us in Christ Jesus from all eternity,"
(II Tim. 1:9 NASB).

Above all things, a minister must have had a definite, life transforming, personal experience with God through His Son, the Lord Jesus Christ. Essentially, he must know God better than he knows his best friend, and although it may seem difficult, better even than his wife, or husband. Unfortunately, this can become an area of contention for many involved in ministry, especially for those who have married someone who has a high degree of need for the attention and time of the minister. Truly, the leaders first love in ministry is for God. Second to the love of God, and flowing from that love, is the love of ones spouse and children. This is not tragic, it is reality, and something that must be considered before one enters into marriage or ministry.

In the end, no amount of training, education, or even Charismatic talent will make up for a deficient spiritual life. Preachers can only live off "past anointing" for so long. God wants His leaders to "be," and then to "do." His goal or priority for His servants is that we would first be all that He created us to be, as men and women in the sight of God, and then to do all that He has called us to do. It is easy in the day-to-day tribulations of life to get these two mixed and out of proper balance.

Remember, being miraculously converted from the degradation of life does not necessarily qualify one to be a spiritual leader in the house of God, either immediately or ultimately. A good testimony is just that: a good testimony. A dynamic testimony is not in and of itself qualification for leadership especially pastoral ministry. Qualification stems from preparation of the heart and character, being filled with the spirit of God in order to function with anointing in the development of spiritual life.

Strong Biblical and Intellectual Life

"A workman who does not need to be ashamed, accurately handling the Word of truth,"
(II Tim. 2:15 NASB).

Many in the Body of Christ read their Bibles. Others who sit in the pew on Sunday mornings, especially in America, are Biblically illiterate. Nevertheless, men or women of God must truly be people of the Book! Leaders must have ingested the word of God, as did the scribes, teachers and prophets in the Old Testament. Jeremiah said, *I ate of His word, and it was sweet.* Leaders must have a deep and abiding relationship with the Living Word, Jesus, and with His written Word, the Bible. For most, three or four years spent in Bible School is only the beginning of the requisite training. Not having attended Bible College should not hamper one from moving into divine gifting and calling. There are many ministers who have never been to Bible school, yet out of deep hunger for God have devoured His Word. They are biblically stronger than many seminary graduates. That, however, is the exception, rather than the rule. Most must go through the time of preparation, depicted throughout the Scriptures as time spent in the wilderness, as illustrated in the story of the children of Israel's forty-year desert sojourn. Preparation in the Word of God should result in transformation of character and the inculcation of His purpose into our hearts and minds.

Our Humanity

As a leader called of God prepares for ministry, they must recognize that involvement in spiritual leadership does not change their basic human needs or remove them from the realm of the human. Men and women, called of God or no, have need of rest, exercise, proper diet, taking care of the physical body (the temple that God has given). We must balance ministry responsibility with family life and recreation, neither of which are incompatible with the call to full time Christian service.

Many within the Body of Christ are convinced that it is their responsibility to keep the leader poor and busy, and the Lord's job to keep the leader humble. Humility *is* a characteristic of the Holy Spirit dwelling in ones life. It is God's plan that all of His children prosper as our soul prospers, not just in finances but in every aspect of life. (II John 2)

Luke 2:52 best illustrates the need of preparation for ministry.

"And Jesus increased in wisdom and stature, and in favor with God and man," (KJV).

If Jesus needed to grow in His preparation before His release into ministry. How much more do potential leaders need to grow as members of His Kingdom. He grew in all aspects of His life, mentally, emotionally, socially, and spiritually. Thus, the leader's preparation is vital.

THOUGHT QUESTIONS

1. A leader's high calling includes several different roles that are to be filled. List at least six of them.
2. Name as many character traits of a shepherd as you can.
3. What is the leader's main focus in life, and why?
4. As we prepare for the ministry, we focus on what three areas of our lives?

Chapter 2
The Leader And Himself

The leader, like any other human being, must live a balanced life to the best of his ability. In life, nothing is more important than health. The body is the temple of the Holy Spirit. If ones body is strong, free of disease, and if the mind is sound, overall function will be better in ministry over the long haul. Tragically, many leaders in the Body of Christ overcome every form of addiction except one or perhaps two; the addiction to food, and the addiction to television or adrenaline.

The latter can be even more insidious than the others. Often what keeps leaders going is the adrenaline rush they feel, called the anointing in many cases, when they preach and teach the Word. They then develop a ravenous hunger, which they satisfy with copious amounts of food, late at night, just before bed. Soon these leaders are struggling with serious physical and emotional problems due to overweight. Their ability to minister effectively can be alarmingly hampered. A leader must evaluate themselves honestly: In what kind of shape am I? Am I really in the shape necessary to make it "over the long haul?"

This was rarely a problem in the Old Testament, although there were a few men who overindulged, i.e., Eli (I Sam. 4:18). Generally, leaders in the Old Testament were men and women of excellent physical condition. In fact, it was required in the Old Testament that the priests be physically perfect to participate in the priesthood. Requirements were strict. Those who were lame, blind, flat-nosed, broken-handed, dwarfed, or scabbed could not minister. Priests could only marry virgins; no widows or divorcees were allowed. Although God has shown grace by using those afflicted, the divine principle of *health* still prevails today. Third John 2 says,

> *"Beloved, I pray that in all respects you may prosper and be in good health, just as your soul*

prospers.." (NASB)

The purpose of physical and emotional health is so that the work of the ministry, which may be filled with late nights, strain, and the burdens of men's souls, will be accomplished. Often leaders are faced with lack of rest, extreme tension, limited opportunity for exercise, and poor eating habits. The very life and strength is easily sapped. For your consideration presented here are six key concerns to address in terms of our physical being.

It is important as ministers of the gospel to develop a balanced life. This is accomplished by firstly avoiding faulty habits such as eating heavy dinners just before bedtime. Moderation in the intake of food and beverage should be the goal. Lots of fruit, vegetables, fresh water help keep the physical body functioning properly. Second, all leaders need an adequate amount of rest. Relaxation and rest are preludes to positive work and worship. Vacations are not a luxury but a necessity in ministry. Complete rest at least one day of each week is needed. Dwight L. Moody took many catnaps. Other men of God have spent time resting every day, in order to remain strong. Third, a good balance of play and exercise is important. Exercise, especially outdoors in fresh air, can rejuvenate ones body and mind. Fourth, much of the ministry is related to the ability to properly speak and see. A heritage of good eyes and an ability to speak well is important. Taking proper care of ones eyes should go without saying. Ignoring vanity and obtaining reading glasses when needed can save much misery. Learning to use the throat in speaking is of obvious importance. Many a preacher has lost his pulpit because he lost his voice. Protecting ones throat and lungs to the best of ones ability shows wisdom. Fifth, any area in the physical realm where a violation of God's principles can provide an open area of attack from Satan. All the prayer in the world will not help on Sunday morning if the leader has been up till three o'clock in the morning preparing a sermon. Unless God has called a leader to a season of prayer, the leader is asking to be terribly fatigued and to perform poorly for God and His people on Sunday morning. Sixth, a spiritual leader should be filled with the joy of the Lord.

JOY FOR THE JOURNEY

"A merry heart does good like a medicine," (Proverbs 17:22 NAS).

Joy and happiness provide strength and vitality. As much as possible, avoid despondency, and despondent people. This in no way means that a leader should avoid those in need of counseling. However, a Pastor must learn how to separate themselves from the counselee to be able to minister effectively. Negative naysayers will eventually drag the best and most positive of leaders down. The joy of the Lord comes through laughter, perhaps through enjoying a funny, "raunch-free" movie, or sharing and enjoying the good things of God with friends who can laugh. Further, joy should come through…

The prayer life of the leader, which is extremely important. Our focus is to daily learning obedience to the Lord, abiding in Him. In prayer, we can learn to lean on the goodness of God, and to hear Him. Also through prayer, we can regularly examine our self. We must use caution and avoid opening doors for little foxes to creep in.

"Catch the foxes for us, The little foxes that are ruining the vineyards, While our vineyards are in blossom." (Song of Solomon 2:15, NAS)

Little foxes, or "small" areas of sin or neglect, begin to destroy the inner man, which can ultimately lead to the destruction of the work of God. Impatience, anger, and pride are faults that preachers condemn from the pulpit, but which often prevail in a minister's life. Watch for these things. To avoid these foxes a leader must be accountable to their spouse, children, and others from outside the local church. A leader must be open to receive input to insure the continuation of positive and productive spiritual growth.

PRIORITIES

In terms of leadership, it is necessary to give oneself solely to the task. It is easy to be caught up in handling the various affairs of running a church, sweeping the church, being the church handyman, driving the bus, etc. It is better to put ten others to work than to do the work of ten. There is no special crown for working oneself to a premature grave. Again, balance is important. Focus on that which is vital; prayer and the ministry of the Word.

As a leader, our primary responsibility is to cast a God breathed vision. God will give vision. Once received, it is necessary to "sell" the vision to others. As the prophet Habakkuk, the leader is to write the vision and make it plain, so that others will read and proclaim it. Speaking the word of life before the people of God to provide vision for them will help keep things in Godly perspective. Eventually, the people God gathers to the leader will take the vision and run with it. It is not enough to just speak it from the pulpit; the leader must also write that vision so that others will read it. When people catch the vision of the leaders' heart, they will become the team members necessary to insure the plans of God will be fulfilled. This, more than anything, is what will give the leader satisfaction with oneself and with the work that God has called us too.

CHARACTER IS KEY

As leaders in the ministry of the Kingdom, we must be careful about our character. It should be without blame. Pastors, as with all leaders, must "practice what we preach." Sadly, hypocrisy in the ministry runs rampant. Those with negative consciences are constantly seeing hypocrisy in their lives. I do not refer to those that genuinely struggle with issues in their life as the Holy Spirit reveals them through God's Word. To continuously allow oneself to be crucified to the flesh is a part of ones daily walk, allowing the spirit-man to grow and mature, thus becoming all that God intended. Frankly, it is more often men than women, who understand that they have characterological flaws, and yet either deny or attempt to explain them away without dealing with them. God will eventually hold every leader accountable for the lifestyle chosen. A self-indulgent lifestyle, devoid of personal holiness, has been the ruin of many a leader.

Thus, the requirement of scripture to build a sound and godly character is a necessary part of preparation for ministry, and the continuation for long term service. Christian character, demonstrated within the local church, and a heart filled with the Spirit of God is a minimum expectation for a leaders life. The following are some of the most important aspects of character strength:

- **Courage**. It takes courage to be ruthless about areas of sin in ones life. A leader must never rehearse or entertain sin. Confess and deal with difficult areas. The mind of a minister is a battleground. The active pursuit of holiness and purity in thought and deed is a daily decision. The leader needs courage to proclaim the gospel and to be a witness to those with whom they reach out to. Courage is required to do what might be unpopular, even if friends are against us.
- **Diligence**. There is no room for slothfulness in the pulpit, nor in the leader's life. Ministry requires hard work and diligence to see a great work come to pass. Redeem the time, for the days truly are evil (Eph. 5:16).
- **Dignity and Poise**. Artificiality or a putting on of airs, acting as the only representative of God on earth, should never be seen in a leader. We are simply leaders in a place of God ordained service. As men and women, called of God, and placed in the Body, God intends to use our specific and specialized gifts for His glory.
- **Contentment**. It is so easy to show discouragement. If the flock one shepherds amounts to thirty or forty people, do

not be discouraged. As a leader is faithful over little, God will make them faithful over much. Most of the great churches in America were overnight successes after fifteen or more years of diligent ministry.
- **Patience**. Leaders deal with people who are trying to make it through life one day at a time. Pastors must be like a parent who recognizes that a child will not mature in a week or two. Children take eighteen, twenty-one, or even more years to come to the fullness of maturity. It is worth the wait, and it is worth the work. Like a nurse, leaders patiently care for the weak or infirm, being sympathetic, tender, discreet, and willing to keep confidences.
- **Forgiveness**. In ministry, it is inevitable that one *will* be sinned against. Rumors will spread, often causing misunderstanding and misrepresentation. Forget about it. If God wants to deal with it, God will do so. Be responsible to forgive quickly, courteously and humbly. Maintaining a teachable spirit will help foster forgiveness.

It is so important that leaders progress as men and women of God in a positive direction. Ones success is not measured by the size of the congregation or by the years of ones ministry. Leaders should always hunger and thirst after God's righteousness, continuously present the gospel for the entirety of life, and avoid the pitfalls that will cause stumbling. These will be covered in Chapter 13, entitled Leaders Pitfalls.

THOUGHT QUESTIONS

1. Leaders are susceptible to which two addictions?
2. God's anointing is sometimes confused with what?
3. List 6 aspects of character strength.
4. How will success in our personal lives NOT be measured? How WILL it be measured?
5. List 5 areas in our lives that will contribute to our success as pastors.

Chapter 3
The Leader and His Family

There could be no greater source of support, or potential heartache, than a spiritual leader's family. The same is true for the family of a pastor. The pressures on pastors and their families can be immense, primarily because of the high expectations placed upon them by both the world and by the church. Unfortunately, the stresses that most effect the family generally come from the church. Some of those pressures are present because the Bible sets certain standards that must be met by any man or woman in leadership in the Body of Christ. But before looking at some of the negative aspects of the ministry and its potential effect upon families, let us look at what the Word of God says about pastoral families.

First, the family should be orderly, not perfect. I Tim. 3:2 and 5 speaks to that. Your congregation may believe that you and your family should be without spot or wrinkle or any such blemish; the Lord, however, requires only that you care your responsibilities well. What really matters is the *managing* of your two-year-old, not his perfection. Two-year-olds are two-year-olds; they act like two-year-olds, regardless of being a pastor's child or not. Thus, be realistic about your children. The same is true about spouses. Pastor's wives are often looked at as associate, almost co-pastors. Unless that job description has been freely chosen by both the pastor and his spouse, that will likely be an unreasonable expectation. God desires that we do the best we can to live out the Christian life and fulfill our obligations in the Lord.

The pastor was called specifically to the ministry, a unique calling. As a man or a woman of God, a Pastor or other Five-fold minister has "heard from the Lord." Usually, the spouse has been called to *you*, not precisely to the ministry. The spouse and the children are not equally called in terms of time or talent. Their gifts, abilities, and desire to use them are simply an extra blessing to the ministry; they are not required, nor are they even the norm for most families.

Third, our **relationship with God does not equal our relationship with the church**. Our ministry must be second to our marriage, which is only subordinated to our relationship to God. This is one of the most difficult areas for most ministers to manage. These are often confused, having such a burning zeal for the ministry that the needs of the spouse and children are neglected in the process. Let me state categorically: Ministry *will* cost something—it always does—but it need not cost ones family. It will be necessary to make adjustments in the family due to the additional time and commitment demanded of a leader. With leadership comes status, improved finances, and other benefits to the rest of the family. Unfortunately, while the corporate CEO and family vacation in Tahiti, the pastor of God's flock might not see immediate financial or other blessings, often leaving a degree of resentment for the family. Again, a wife that feels totally neglected by her husband can become easily embittered to the church and to the ministry. Children may feel neglected, emotionally abandoned by a father who does not regard them as important assets in his life. Beware: Your children are very much part of the ministry, and will remain so with proper planning, prayer, and setting of godly priorities.

Col. 3:18-21 gives insight and wisdom.

> *"Wives, be subject to your husbands, as is fitting in the Lord. Husbands, love your wives, and do not be embittered against them. Children, Be obedient to your parents in all things, for this is well-pleasing to the Lord. Fathers, do not exasperate your children, that they may not lose heart,"*
> **(NAS).**

If a leader is not yet married, they may be looking for a certain type of spouse, and have certain expectations for marriage. Let us look at some further details about the pastor and family life, (and since the general rule is that the pastor will be male, thus the emphasis) beginning with an examination of the characteristics of "the ideal wife."

Proverbs 19:14 says, *"A prudent wife is from the Lord."* The single pastor may find himself in a precarious situation, for many times women will come to the church of a single male pastor with the singular goal of winning his heart and his hand in marriage. The power of the man of God or the prestige of his position draws women to him. Caution and significant prayer (and fasting most likely) should be before dating and making the ultimate decision to marry.

When involving oneself in courtship and marriage, it is important to remember a few interesting points. First of all, over 50% of the success of a marriage depends upon the wife. A percentage of the success of a ministry will also depend upon the wife. Men's egos are on the line, as it were, as they minister from the pulpit. A supportive, soothing, loving wife can make a major difference for even the most godly men.

Secondly, a pastor cannot afford to fall in love merely from a feeling standpoint. The ultimate in foolishness would be to leave your head on the shelf; it is best to use sound reason in courtship and marriage. It is often in the leading of the heart, which according to Jer. 17:9 is desperately wicked, that any man or woman can make a tragic mistake.

Thus, the individual that is chosen to court and certainly marry should be spiritual, educated, and able to be a partner in some aspect of the ministry. Clarification of this premise is necessary to avoid possible misunderstanding or seeming contradiction. Everyone in the Body of Christ has certain gifts, talents, and abilities. This will certainly be true of the Pastors spouse, and later the children. For example, in my home, my wife did not play the piano well enough to perform, she did not sing well enough to lead the choir, nor was she comfortable in the role of teacher or preacher. But she was very gifted in the area of general administration and financial management. She was able to alleviate a tremendous burden from me in this area of the ministry.

Similarly, my daughters were and are able to teach. They have been actively involved in Sunday School teaching, church life and para-church ministries. They have their own gifts and abilities, and are using them to the glory of God, as they are currently able. Will a wife *never* be able to teach or function in other areas of ministry? Perhaps, perhaps not, depending upon two factors, her, and God. God is willing to take us farther than we ever want to go, without violating our free will. He wants us to function well and *enjoy* our life in Christ and in the Family.

When considering a potential spouse, be careful to consider character. A wife should be intensely spiritual. Her life is also a ministry to the congregation. She becomes the mother, as it were, of the church. She must complement the spiritual leaders life. If she is extremely weak, emotionally or mentally, she will need strengthening before marriage, because of the incredible stresses of ministry.

She needs to be a woman who can be **content with change.** It is very rare that a pastor will take a ministry and remain thirty, forty, or fifty years in the same place. Most ministries and ministers move on occasion. If she is unwilling to change locations, she can create tremendous difficulty in terms of ministry progression. She should be kind and hospitable. The word "hospitable" needs to be defined to include mutual respect between the pastor's family and guests. None should feel free to just drop into pastor's house whenever they feel like it, or disturb dinner five days in a row! Nevertheless, a wife should be able to show proper care and kindness to the *whosoever will* that may come to their house.

She also must be clearly consecrated, set aside for the work of service. She serves first her husband and children, and secondarily, those in the church. Duties may be thrust upon her simply because she is the wife of the pastor. These duties can include, and are not limited to;

- Pinch-hitting in preaching if no one else is available. The hope is that any minister's spouse would be able to

- at least teach if called upon in time of emergency.
- Visitation, or being able to minister effectively to other women, especially the younger in the Body of Christ. She may assist needy women in their areas of difficulty.
- Giving advice. In fact, women *will* call upon her, assuming her spiritual authority and knowledge, whether true or not.
- Assisting as a hostess and taking care of details for her husband, especially if he's forgetful.
- Being part of various church programs.
- Assisting at altar calls, weddings, funerals, etc.

All of these can be duties of any pastor's spouse. Again, the expectations should be modulated by the strengths and abilities of that spouse. A wife should not be pressured into fulfilling any or all of these roles. She should be willing to embrace them as necessary or as she is able. To re-emphasize, a wife's primary duties are to her family, to supply a tremendous amount of support for her husband in leadership. She can best uphold him through private prayer and intercession, as well as through love and affection. Being a positive influence through smiles and public support can be a great blessing. The gift of encouragement is vitally needed, especially for men in positions of godly responsibility. On Sunday Pastors preach their hearts out with a hope and expectation that God will move in some significant way. Usually, it is on the same given Sunday that the greatest complaints about the church or ones leadership style is registered. The worst day of the week, then, seems to be Monday. It helps to have a supportive, encouraging spouse who will listen solicitously as the leaders heart is openly sharing, perhaps bitterly complaining. Note this, spouses: The spiritual leader is only human, and is just complaining. Do not take all of these complaints seriously. It does not mean that the desire to resign is a true threat or thought through intention. It is helpful to have a wise wife who can give advice and feedback to her husband that no one else may be willing to give. I still remember an occasion when I was preaching in Connecticut.

About halfway through a serious sermon, my lovely wife, who was sitting in the congregation, began to laugh. After the service, I took Karen to the side and asked, "My goodness, woman, what were you laughing at?" Again bursting into laughter, she finally told me that she had been looking at my face. I said, "Wonderful. You don't like the way my face looks." She said, "No! I was noticing your mustache (which I proudly wore for many years)." She continued, "Your mustache is white on one side and white on the other side, and black in only one spot in the middle. It looked like you had something disgusting hanging underneath your nose!" I shaved off that mustache the very next day.

In many cases a wife has a wonderful gift of intuition. She is able to hear and sense the undercurrents in a congregation. She is able to perceive ill intention toward her husband, and can especially sense if someone of the opposite sex has purulent interest. As husbands, let us appreciate her gift of intuition and heed the warnings that come from a loving and submitted spouse. Husbands need to love, honor, and respect their wives, in public, in private, and especially in front of their children. Because leaders and their families are public figures, they are privy to much information. So often pastors can feel overburdened with the information. Therefore it is good to include the spouse and children (when they are old enough and mature enough to handle the information) in what is going on in church life.

A minister's family can be somewhat lonely. They might miss their husband and father because of board meetings, deacon's meetings, elder's meetings, Wednesday night service, etc. Make special time for the family. Whenever possible, help around the house and assist in the day-to-day cares of family life. Be interested in what is happening in the families day.

Male leaders must learn to honor their wives at church. People expect it. If flowers or cards are never given, others will notice the lack of appropriate tenderness. Leaders should also be polite with their spouses, opening doors for them, helping them with their coat, etc. This shows a positive model and helps maintain the romance in the marital relationship. The wife should not have to raise the family and live a public life all by herself. She should know that she does have a loving and supportive spouse who will help carry the load.

Thus, giving time to ones spouse and children is a way to model how a positive and loving relationship should flow in the Christian home. The spouse is the most important ally in the life of ministry.

Women require security. Provide it, to the best of your ability. This may not be so easy when one is just starting out in ministry. That is why a plan for the future should be developed together. Wherever possible, include medical insurance for the whole family in a compensation plan. Provide a home that becomes the families as part of a compensation package. Make sure that the family does not have to survive solely on the gifts provided by the congregation.

Of course, many of the items in this discussion will not hold true for one in their first pastorate, or when just beginning in ministry. All leaders will suffer to a certain extent as part of service to the Lord. One should at least begin with a plan for providing for a family. Recognize that ones spouse, as a co-laborer with the pastor, should be cared for to the best of ones ability.

The care of a household means more than just providing for and protecting the family. It also includes caring for the children. Children can be the parents' greatest joy, or the greatest problem, which is true of any family, unsaved and Christian alike. It is especially true in a pastor's family. According to the Scripture, a leaders household must be well ordered. This does not include an attempt to create perfect children, but to love and discipline them so that they can grow just like any other child. It is true that leaders children live in a fishbowl of sorts, ogled at by the outside world. Nevertheless, it is imperative that they be protected while at the same time encouraging them to be whole and complete people.

Not every pastor will have the finest of homes. What the leader does have should be kept neat, a place of open hospitality. At the same time, recognize the security and privacy needs of the family. It is helpful to be an active participant in the development of family life. The pastor and family usually become primary entertainers for visiting missionaries, evangelists, and traveling teachers. Plan ahead for these visits, and yet, it is unwise to make ones family visitors in their own home. It might be better for the church to pay for a hotel, rather than pushing a child from his bedroom which will likely communicate to him that his needs do not matter. Thus the pastor's home should be a place of warmth and love, just as any other Christian family's, at the same time recognizing the special needs and concerns that must be attended to as a spiritual leader.

Conclusion

It will take wisdom and certain work to insure that our ministry will be a blessing to our family.

Life in ministry can be most difficult, often even cruel. One famous leader whose name escapes me stated that if one can do anything else but preach, by all means do it. There is little glamour for most in ministry, few monetary rewards, few accolades for great service. All true spiritual leaders have a focus on an eternal crown. However, there are important temporal items that we must tend to insure the completion of ones journey for the King and His Kingdom.

THOUGHT QUESTIONS

1. The Bible presents certain standards that the pastor and his family should meet. Briefly outline them, and give references.
2. List some of the qualities to look for in a wife.
3. How can the pastor encourage and bless his wife?
4. What particular danger may present itself to a single pastor?

Chapter 4
The Leader and His Church

Students, especially those having a desire for pastoral ministry, will eventually face the challenge of the first church or ministry assignment. How the new leader functions within their first church assignment will often determine the effectiveness of the rest of their ministry.

There are several points that must be considered before looking more intently at the first church that a pastor will take as a minister of the gospel.

First, it is important to remember *Whose* church one is going to be pastoring. Jesus is the Head of the Church (Col. 1:18).

Again, Jesus said in Mat. 16:18,

"I will build My Church, and the gates of Hell will not prevail against it."

Jesus is more invested in His Church than any leader of the church could ever be. The Church was on his mind and heart before the world began (Eph. 1:4). The Church is not an afterthought; it is central to the very plan and purpose of God. Thus, when thinking of the church universal and its local expression, it should be remembered that it is a most divinely instituted instrument, created for the propagation of the gospel and for the care of the saints. Therefore, as discussed in chapter 1, leaders have an important fiduciary responsibility for the care and stewardship of God's house.

Secondly, and most importantly, whenever accepting an assignment, especially a new position, or make a new start, it is just that, an opportunity for a brand new beginning. One must always remember (unless involved in a church plant with primarily new converts, which has its own set of problems to be discussed later), there is an inheriting of another's legacy that must be carefully considered and navigated. Without question, people become intensely loyal to their pastors, even interim pastors, who have been shepherding the local church. Many may be delighted about a new pastor taking leadership and providing new opportunity for fellowship, but many will be naturally suspicious about the motivations and abilities of the "new kid on the block." Even the most sincere and charismatic of leaders will have their loyalty to the churches needs, desires, and wishes seriously questioned. Behind every new church or ministry assignment is a great deal of history. Familiarizing oneself with its intricacies could save much heartache and potential embarrassment. Unless it is a brand new church plant, the key to success could be in the roots of the church. Eventually, the new pastor will also become a part of the church's history, hopefully in a positive sense.

Whether a younger or older minister, move into a first or new pastoral assignment with eyes wide open. Learn as much as possible about that local assembly, first, before making any radical changes which will disturb the sheep. In reality, people are very much like sheep. They are easily frightened by change. They like to graze in the same place they have grazed for years. They are not accustomed to new and different forms or styles of worship. Therefore, a leader must start where people are, slowly drawing them to the place to which the new leader senses God wants for the congregation. This will help the new pastor to avoid frightening the sheep, which can cause tremendous heartache and significant problems.

When moving into a first church, a pastor will often find themselves replacing a retiring pastor or a pastor who has just left that local church. In all situations, and this is part of good ministerial ethics, it is important to honor his or her name and ministry. Do not criticize their methods or their results. It is good to keep in mind:

> *"Then the King of Israel answered and said, Tell him, 'Let not him who girds on his armor boast like he who takes it off,"* (I Kings 20:11 NAS).

Simply speaking, it is always unwise to think of oneself more highly than one ought. As a new pastor, thinking that all of the answers to all of their prayers has arrived is ludicrous. No matter how the past leadership has been, it is wrong to provide or entertain a comparison to the old pastor, until one has ridden in the harness for a season.

Also, do not try to make major changes too quickly. New plans may be much better than what the old plans were, and the new vision may be exactly what the local fellowship needs. Yet, if one presents new plans and vision too quickly, it will likely frighten people away. If at all possible, receive advice with an open heart and mind from the retiring pastor. Hopefully, the retiring pastor will not disclose all the untoward secrets about the lives of the members of the congregation. Generally, a pastor does not want or need to know those secrets, since they are interpretations filtered through the experiences of that one former pastor. A Pastor must have the opportunity to build new and meaningful relationships with God's people without bias or rancor. As a leader, one has ample opportunity to learn of the special quirks of the members of the local ministry.

It is important to have a good beginning. Hopefully the retiring pastor will be there to help make the transition a smooth and positive one (if he has been voted out of the church for some reason, you will certainly want to question why you are going to that place to begin with). Once the retiring pastor is through with his final official duties, it is important that he cut his ties to that congregation wherever possible, and move away from that local church. That doesn't necessarily mean that he must move out of the community, but he must have the ministerial ethics to cut the ties, so that when people have problems with the new leader...yes, that is likely to happen...they won't be tempted to contact the former pastor to receive "counsel." This is contrary to the smooth and healthy transition needed in the local fellowship. It is best to dialogue about all this and make decisions about it a long time before entering into the role of a pastor in a new parish setting.

Also, recognize that people are looking to their new leader

to lead. Confidence as a leader will not be tremendous in the beginning. Since the new Pastor is just beginning to know the people to whom one is ministering, there will be some natural tentativeness. Thus, as a leader, counting the cost of entering into this new position and assuring oneself, as well as those in the congregation, that a commitment to lead can be made without reservation is essential. The congregation will likely ask themselves if their pastor is in this ministry for the duration. This question is of greater significance if one is following a pastor who has been there for five or more years. The people have become used to a certain pastoral leadership style. Yet they are more than willing, in most cases, to receive fresh leadership. They need to be reassured that the new leadership has every intention of making a true go of it.

Let me illustrate this by relating an incident of transition in my own ministry. The following is an illustration of a move made by the author.

"When I took the reins of our International Bible College Network, I was less than confident. The previous leadership had been significantly more charismatic, gifted in gathering others around him.

My self-doubt was only too apparent. I was blessed to receive counsel and encouragement from a Pastor's Pastor (and Vision International University alumnus), Dr. David Wyns. David stated, 'You are the leader—just lead and others will follow.' With some trepidation, I stepped into the fray, and God has helped us as by faith I have led with strength and determination."

Again, as a new leader it is imperative that one move slowly, according to the abilities that God has given, and the temperament of the congregation or ministry. Confidence in ones ability to lead will be bolstered through seeking the Lord and finding a unique pattern for effective ministry. It is also helpful, if at all possible, to have outside counsel with men and women whom are trustworthy, mentors that will assist in the handling of the difficulties inherent in any new beginning.

A Team

One of the initial goals upon entering a new or first pastorate is cooperation. It is vital to gain the cooperation of the leaders who are already stationed within that local fellowship. This is not always an easy accomplishment. It takes wisdom to build positive and mutually beneficial relationships. Some will not like their new pastor simply because they will not like any new pastor. Obviously, wisdom would dictate that they would not be a positive addition to your leadership team. Depending upon the government of the fellowship, a leader may have to tolerate men and women who see themselves as devil's advocates (as though the devil needs any advocates!) As a leader in a new situation, the avoidance of premature endorsements until having first labored with them for a season is self-evident. By observing the character of a man or woman under fire, you will be best able to determine who will serve well in leadership.

Further, a new minister should be willing to meet townspeople and become visible within the community.

The focus is to involve as many people as possible within the local fellowship. Even if a pastor could delegate every administrative responsibility, and truly focus exclusively on prayer and the preaching and teaching of the Word, one would still find themselves intensely busy.

It is very important as one enters into a new leadership position, especially as a pastor, that all the details of daily life be outlined, in terms of what the fellowship expects of you. Do they have expectations regarding visitation, phone calls, or office hours? What are their emphasis in terms of ministry or specific doctrinal stances, what is the complete salary package, what is the organizational structure of the local church, and what are the rights as a pastor in terms of selecting ones own leadership team. All of these things are a part of weighing the cost before entering into a first pastorate. If the leader fails to deal with these matters up front, they will eventually come back to haunt the pastoral experience.

Be careful not to take oneself too seriously! The saying fits:

Don't sweat the small stuff. It's *all* small stuff, except the spiritual matters, those things that are really important in the life of any individual. A birth, a death, an illness, the need for spiritual counsel and guidance, those are the weighty matters. Whether Brother Whatsit liked the color of Pastors tie or enjoyed the singing of Sister Whippendittle is not vital. The spiritual leader will be dealing with these things; just don't take them too seriously.

OTHER TIPS

When beginning a tenure at a new local church, do not put all of the best and most dynamic messages up front. Sprinkle them out over the first year or so. The listeners will always be excited about something new and fresh as it comes their way.

In terms of relationship with the people of God in a first pastorate, remember that the pastor is a friend of man and a minister of God. Have a genuine love for the people of God and for those that are needy and "unlovely." A pastor is an example for the flock; be willing, then, to reach out and touch others who are hurting. Showing love and compassion is an out-growth of God's unique call as a pastor.

Refrain from putting on airs especially in the pulpit. There will always be better preachers. Preaching does lift the preacher above the mundane, however it is helpful to be at least related to the same person in the pulpit as out. The people will recognize you as being a genuine human being. Preachers often make the mistake of putting on an entirely different voice, a completely new persona. Their entire style changes. They then revert to "normal" when they step down from the pulpit. It makes it difficult for people to properly relate to such a lofty person.

Also, demonstrating a zeal for God through ones personal prayer life and devotion to the Lord is vital. Eventually, the people of God the pastor is shepherding will bond with their shepherd, and will emulate their leader. Thus our spiritual stance and moral integrity is the most important sermon that the people will ever hear.

Because the average pastor is two-thirds pastor and one-third preacher, the resident pastor will never need to fear a visiting minister's great oratory. No evangelist can really take the place of a true shepherd. In reality, the people will learn to love their own shepherd's voice. Though the local pastor may not be the greatest preacher in the world; that will not matter to the people of God. If the leader will love God's people sincerely and minister to their needs through every cycle of life, the loyalty and love will be returned. The shepherd's feeling of their pain, assisting them in times of difficulty, and being there for them in the trials of life is what matters more than how great a preacher they may or may not be.

Finally, it is important to have a clear understanding of basic human nature. Everyone is a psychologist. Some are trained and some are not. No one expects a pastor to know everything about human behavior, but a leader should, to the best of ones ability, be fascinated with each member of the flock that God has given. Learn about their common needs and their individual quirks. Jesus rubbed shoulders with farmers and fishermen, publicans and politicians, with the very rich and the very poor during His life and ministry. He lived with men of honor and women of dishonor, as well as all points in-between. We must be willing to follow His lead as our supreme Leader.

Ultimately, there will be a continual need to work on simple skills. Like remembering people's names, maintaining ones smile, listening for another's viewpoint without needing to constantly prove that the leader is right (a sure sign of insecurity). Remain optimistic about people's problems, even though they may seem unanswerable. All of life boils down to a walk of faith. Pastors are called to walk alongside of those to whom we minister in pastoral care. Do necessary corrections with humility and meekness, not openly to prove ones power, but in a true spirit of love.

Pastoral ministry is a tremendous challenge in the best of circumstances. With God's help, a large dose of humility and grace, and the gifts that the Lord has provided, the church and flock will grow and mature to the Glory of God.

THOUGHT QUESTIONS

1. Name at least 6 important points to remember before taking your first pastorate.
2. You will want to quickly accomplish several initial goals as you move into your first pastorate. Name at least one of them.
3. You are a minister of God and a friend of man. As such, what genuine attributes (also God's attributes) must you demonstrate to others?
4. The average pastor is a certain percentage pastor and a certain percentage preacher. Give the percentages and explain why this information will relieve a pastor's fears of a visiting minister's exceptional preaching skills.

Chapter 5
The Leader and His Pulpit

The first pulpit for any individual pastor can be rife with difficulties. If approached with wisdom, and a sense of adventure, it can be a most exiting and rewarding season of ministry.

Many say that the place of greatest influence for the local pastor is the pulpit. One could not find a better arena for communicating personal thoughts, beliefs, and opinions, than that of a gathering of people in a local church. The preacher of the gospel of Jesus Christ focuses on communicating the truth of God's word from the pulpit. The pastor preaches as the oracle of God; his own opinions about God and His people, or the climate in which we live, can be discussed in another forum. That is, a preacher is not to just speak out of his own mind, but hopefully is inspired out of the fire of the Holy Spirit. Thus, a pastor preaching the Word of God is a man/woman with a message, spoken as the mouthpiece of God. The spiritual leader is to speak with the authority of a prophet as one brings forth the "thus saith the Lord." A "flame of fire" should come forth from the very bones of every preacher. That flame needs to be rekindled regularly in the pastor's prayer closet. We have discussed this earlier, and it will be reiterated in our final chapter.

There is no replacement for the anointed fire of God coming through the mouth of a preacher. At the same time, it must be balanced with a clearly thought out and prepared message, in order that the truth will be presented palatably to the people who listen. Nothing more greatly offends the sensibilities than hearing someone void of an understanding of a message from God, and yet filled with, as Dr. Ken Chant says, the "froth and bubble" of an orator out of control. Preaching is not about yelling, singing away a song that makes no sense, or stirring only the emotions. True preaching must have the zeal of God, coming forth as a message which can be understood and applied to the lives of those who listen.

The preparation to preach is the preparation of a life. A sermon is not born in the study of it alone. It is grown and nurtured through the spiritual life of the preacher. One's sermons are the fruit of a life spent in relationship with God. Regularly praying oneself into the mood to preach and then leaving it all behind Sunday night is a ticket to an eventual fall. Preaching is the result of a continuous abiding relationship with Christ and a sweet and wonderful communion with God. Thus, the responsibility of a preacher is to preach the Word of God.

"Preach the word; be ready in season and out of season; reprove, rebuke, exhort, with great patience and instruction," **(II Tim. 4:2 NAS).**

A minister must live in the Word of God.

Ultimately, a pastor is a Bible man. One great preacher stated, "We should not just have our nose stuck in a Bible." This man spends half his time in the Bible, and the other half in the newspaper. He is thus able to take the truth of God's word and apply it to the real life scenarios facing people on a daily basis. He brings the Word to bear in the daily life of the believer. A regular time for study and meditation should be an active part of ones spiritual walk. Much of Bible reading is casual, not as intense as the search for a sermon. Out of the full reading of the Scripture will come those God-given thoughts that eventually become messages. Teachers regularly advise students to prepare messages, even on the weeks they are not scheduled to preach. Always prepare one to three messages every week. The preparation of a series of messages can be a blessing to the Pastor and the congregation. One never knows when the opportunity will arise to bring forth the Word in time and season.

What is it that pastors preach? Of course, they preach sermons. A sermon is a part of life filled with the unction of the Holy Spirit, rooted and grounded in the Word of God. A pastors focus in preaching the sermon is to feed the sheep. Sermons filled with heavy theological content from previous or present Bible College Education are wonderful...if one is teaching a Bible College class. However, these messages are not always applicable in a local fellowship. Messages dealing with the practical aspects of life are more germane. Yet, a preacher should not be afraid to tackle some of the weightier issues; the issue of sin, the need for salvation, the blood of Jesus, heaven and hell. These tremendous topics are often overlooked in today's pulpits.

A sermon is as long as it is good. If fifteen minutes puts an audience to sleep, do not preach one moment longer. If a preacher has the ability to captivate people for forty-five minutes or more, go for it. A well constructed, thirty to thirty-five minute sermon is usually more than adequate to fill the people of God with both inspiration and information applicable to life.

Every sermon should move the hearers closer to a relationship with the Lord. Thus, weave Christ, His cross, death and resurrection into virtually every sermon. Ultimately, every sermon should present the righteousness of God, the peace of Christ, and the joy of the Holy Spirit; the Kingdom of God. A leader may use oneself as an example, without losing the central person of Christ in the sermon. Thus the greatest compliment a pastor should receive is not what a great preacher one is, but, "How I was touched by God! What a great God we serve!"

Sermons should be clear. Do not attempt to preach the sermons of men loftier than the preacher. Deeper teaching and life messages are only good if one is able to teach them with great clarity. Thus, simplicity without being simplistic, is much more important than complexity. The goal is to feed the sheep, to move them a step closer in their relationship with God, and to aid them in surviving their week with greater grace and victory. Come down to earth in preaching. Leave the great theories and speculations for those of greater intellect. Intellectual debates are rarely helpful to the common man. They want, need and deserve to hear the Word of God presented palatably.

All sermons should be preached in earnest. They should demonstrate the time and energy spent in their development.

People want their pastor to give it all that they have, to fill it with emotion, pictures, color, lights, whatever necessary to bring it to a vivid conclusion. Ones sermons should move people to a decision for Christ. There is always a place for evangelism, teaching, exhortation, prophesy, comfort, reproof, and doctrine; all of these are important and should be scattered throughout the teaching and preaching of the Word. Be willing to vary the style of preaching. The rut of pet themes and subjects leads to an anemic local church. How does one develop great teaching and preaching? First, it starts in the pastors study. The servant of God must study God's Word and the current events of the day. Opening ones mind to continuous learning, never becoming static. Properly mix Bible study and prayer. Both are essential for readiness to give a word in time and season.

Certain thoughts will come to mind as books and papers are read, while watching the television (but be careful of the potential trap of receiving all input from this medium), or interacting with the children. Take notes! Jot down thoughts that occur during these relatively passive times and keep a good file of them. Go to the library and gather information about certain topics. Be versed on the wonderful tools available to leaders today, such as America on Line, CompuServe, CD-ROM's, and specialized computer programs that can help in personal study. Even with these wonderful inventions, they will do little good if they are never used. It takes a commitment of time and energy to gather the information that will help in preaching an effective sermon.

Make notes as the sermon is being prepared. There is nothing wrong with preparing sermon notes. The difficulty comes if the preacher becomes totally tied to them. Some would preach incoherently if they happened to lose a page, or become unable to complete the sermon. Thus, one should not be locked into their notes, though note-taking can be very effective for several reasons. First, notes can help the preacher remember where one is in the middle of preaching a sermon. Even the greatest of orators have been know to follow a rabbit trail, only to be brought back on track by well prepared and handy notes. Two, they help in the organization of the preachers thoughts for clarity of presentation. Just wandering through what seems to be inspirational material in front of the congregation can hardly be seen as preaching. For some, there are specific note-taking plans that they like to use. Many will use handy eight and one half by eleven pieces of paper for their notes. I always like to keep files of previous sermons. Often, I will preach at a different church and find no need to recreate the wheel; I just modify what I have already worked on.

As a preacher, of course, part of the ministry is to preach evangelistically. The scripture indeed states that all preachers are to do the work of an evangelist. Pastors should not depend upon evangelists alone to bring soul-winning messages; that is part of every pastors responsibility. The heart of the church is evangelism. The cry of a leaders heart should be that God would give more souls. Thus, there should be an entire emphasis on evangelism, occasionally preaching evangelistically from the pulpit.

Every church goes through highs and lows, ups and downs. Each needs times of revival. Perhaps one is gifted enough to continuously stir the flame of revival in the hearts of God's people. For most pastors, however, it is helpful, even essential, to rely upon the rest of the Five-Fold Ministry. Those with apostolic call and gifting help to lay foundations, prophets bring forth a "thus saith the Lord," to take us, as Prophet Kim Clement said, "Out of today into tomorrow." Further, as with all Five-fold ministry, the Prophet is to equip God's people for maturity. The evangelist ministers primarily for the salvation of souls, and equips the People of God as soul winners, and the pastors disciple the flock. At times there is a need for gifted teachers who can nourish a spiritual growth spurt with a solid teaching ministry.

Evangelistic preaching and occasional outside revivals are needed. It is not just emotionalism; it is literally to stir God's people to a spirit of evangelism, so that the reaching of the community with the gospel of Jesus Christ is possible. Soul winning is born out of intercessory prayer and from a deep hunger to see others saved through the knowledge of Jesus Christ.
Pastors will be doing a significant amount of teaching. Thus at

least one good message during the week should be devoted to fundamental teaching. Strong saints must be fed as well as exercised. Pastors may lose fruit because they prune and plow, and forget to teach and nurture. Bringing in others with Five-Fold Gifting can assist where the Pastor may be weak.

Preaching the declaration of the Evangel, the good news of Jesus Christ is what most preachers love to do. If this were not true, the call to full-time Christian service must be questioned. It can be the most exhilarating, and at times the most frustrating, of all endeavors. No matter how anointed one feels, how well prepared and delivered the sermons, there is always the human element. Pastors must remember that many of the prophets who were obviously anointed of God, set aside for great purpose and tremendously gifted orators, received little or no reward for their effort. Why? They preached to hard-hearted, hard-headed, deaf-eared men and women who rather enjoyed darkness for a season than the light of God for eternity.

Thus, if preaching does not receive immediate response or recognition with a great flood of souls streaming to the altar or prayer room, do not be discouraged. All preachers and ministries experience highs and lows. It is faithfulness over time that equates to successful ministry. Dynamic preaching will impact someone during each day. In fact, it is often the message that in retrospect feels the least effective that makes the most significant impact. The preacher never knows how much impact. It is impossible to determine if a sermon was just the seed necessary to inspire another to greatness. As one preaches God's Word, they must preach with a focus that *Yes, they will hear, yes, they will believe, yes, they will receive.* Preach with faith. Plow in hope, and expect that, based upon God's Word, there *will* be fruit that will remain. So in preaching do not be weary in well-doing. In due season a faithful servant of the Lord *will* reap a reward if you do not faint (Gal. 6:9).

THOUGHT QUESTIONS

1. The preacher needs to keep in mind what important fact as he preaches?
2. Why prepare sermons every week, even if not scheduled to preach?
3. What is the focus of preaching?
4. Why should you occasionally bring in an outside revival?

Chapter 6
The Leader and His Friends

As with corporate Chief Executive Officers, it is often quite lonely at the top. It is not unusual for the pastor to have friendly relationships with only his immediate family. This is partially due to the difficulty of finding a confidant within one's own church or parish. In fact, very few deacons or elders have the maturity for hearing the deep desires and difficulties of pastoral life without becoming critical or judgmental toward their spiritual leader. It is said that *familiarity breeds contempt*. It certainly seems true regarding the ministry, for people tend to place pastors and their families on a higher pedestal than anyone else in society. Parishioners look to their pastor as their spiritual leader and source of the continuity of life. Any sign of perceived weakness therefore may create difficulties. Yet, the deep need for friendships for pastors and their families remains, though potential dangers lurk. Let me give you an example.

Many years ago I counseled a pastor and his family who were experiencing a difficult transitional adjustment. They had made a long move, which was exacerbated by a new cultural setting. They were hundreds of miles from home, with little or no actual friends within their community. One day, in the process of sharing his frustrations with another pastor in his district, my pastor friend said, "Sometimes I feel like cashing it all in and going home."

That statement must have pushed some sort of button (the wrong kind). His so-called friend spread the information. Literally within days, the church began to receive resumes of pastoral candidates looking for an opportunity to pastor the church that my friend had "vacated." In reality, he had only made a statement while discouraged, a frequent occurrence amongst friends. It was taken and spread like gossip and wildfire, causing a tremendous stir within that church and none-too-little consternation and pain to my friend and his family. Thus, while it is important that we all choose and cultivate friendships based upon *mutual trust* within the Body of Christ, it is especially true of pastors.

Pastors are givers. They are listeners, giving of their time, energy, and heart. Often, they develop friendships that are based upon the needs of others that come to them, which are rarely the most healthy of relationships. In fact, pastors need to find friendships with other pastors, business leaders, or other professionals, preferably Christian, with whom they can share their heart, have fun, and play games during their non-church time; friendships holding little to no risk of personal exposure and pain. This must be a priority for most pastors since they become so locked into the work to which God has called them. A friendship outside of one's local church is one way to keep a positive balance. Whenever in town, it is helpful to enjoy a weekly racquetball game or other sport with a friend. When done on a regular basis the fellow player he has can become a dear family friend, especially if they are not directly connected with the ministry or church. With a true friend, one can share many things, and a closeness can be developed over time. It is safe and comfortable, and will not jeopardize the leader professionally or personally. This friend can also become a prayer warrior. As you share hearts together, a relationship such as this can become very precious.

Friendships are extremely important. It is strongly encouraged for every pastor to look for similar close friendships and accountable relationships outside their own church, and even outside their denominational affiliation. In this manner they can continue to develop a rounded personality and have the opportunity to speak their heart and unburden themselves in a safe and a caring manner.

THOUGHT QUESTIONS

1. What is one danger of friendships for a pastor?
2. Upon what must a pastor's friendships be based?
3. Where are good places a pastor can look for friendships?
4. Why do pastors need friendships?

Chapter 7
The Leader and His Time

God requires of every leader, especially those in pastoral ministry, to utilize their time to the best of their ability, in order to ensure that they can fulfill God's mandate for their life. Time is an interesting phenomenon that only applies to human beings. Time, as we know it, does not exist in the spirit realm. God is above all time, unlimited by time, place, and person. He has placed our world under significant time constraints; twenty-four hours in a day, seven days in a week. Most of us, if truly blessed, will have between 40 and as many as 60 years to labor. Forty years seems to the young virtually an eternity, to the middle-aged, it seems woefully short, and to those in their 60's and later years, it seems as though life has come and gone in a flash. God gave time, which can be viewed as a curse or a gift. Pastors with wisdom will see time as a gift from the Lord, but one that has distinct constraints and parameters by which one must learn to live.

In every twenty-four hour period, most people need between seven and eight hours to sleep. The rest of the day is used for rest, recreation, eating, communication, and work. In most western states, an eight hour day with an hour for lunch and two fifteen minute breaks, is a "normal" workday. Those parameters do not apply to most ministers of the gospel. In fact, for most successful people, it takes an average of fifty hours a week to accomplish goals of growth and productivity.

Time must be managed. Every pastor must be aware of the latest and best methods for managing time, in order to function well in his or her pastoral role. Certainly, nothing but the spiritual functions of ministry should take first place, but the other roles often attempt to crowd the time available for adequate ministry.

Each leader must establish adequate boundaries to ensure that they will not be encroached upon negatively by congregational needs. In order to do that, one must be prayerful, mindful of a balanced life and how to establish it. Thus leaders must seek God earnestly for a plan for effective time management.

Time management can be coined as the pastor's calendar. The Word of God states a great deal about time and its usage. Pastors do not answer to a time clock; therefore they must learn to discipline, or redeem the time that God has provided, recognizing its shortness.

Ps. 90:12 states,

"So teach us to number our days, that we may apply our hearts unto wisdom."

Having an appointment book that one actually uses on a regular basis is a first step. Secondly, keep proper priorities.

"But this I say, brethren, the time has been shortened, so that from now on those who have wives should be as though they had none; and those who weep, as though they did not weep; and those who rejoice, as though they did not rejoice; and those who buy, as though they did not possess," **(I Cor. 7:29-30 NAS).**

Third, focus on the task at hand.

"See then that you walk circumspectly, not as fools, but as wise, redeeming the time, for the days are evil," **(Eph. 5:15-16).**

Let us look at some practical hints to help Gods' leader manage the day, ones time, and ones family life.

First, keep a daily diary of activities and a date book. As much as possible, schedule the most important activities, the first priority being time alone with God. Secondly, schedule time with your family. Third, allocate time for study and prayer. Fourth would be church business, with the people of the church being first, rather than paperwork. Fifth, make sure that recreation, rest and exercise is planned for, and finally, schedule time for friends. Each night before retiring, a leader should review the progress for that day, and plan the schedule for the following day. Put everything in writing. Most pastors have relatively good memories, but why trust them? It is fairly easy to forget the "things that we really wanted to forget to begin with;" having to visit certain people that tend to get under ones skin. Therefore writing down key appointments and commitments is very important.

Be realistic about how the schedule for the day is developed. There are only so many hours in it! One way to ensure a realistic schedule is to share it with ones spouse and children, and note their feedback. Check also with one or two pastors who have learned to schedule and manage their time well. They may be able to provide some helpful hints in terms of priorities and better utilization of time. Ask for help if the day is getting out of control.

The pastor MUST set his priorities in the ministry. Each pastor is constantly forced into making decisions. Some of them may be minor, but some will have lasting effects on the ministry, the pastor and his family. Priorities needing to be considered first seem to be the most difficult to get a handle on. Pastoring should not be just a day-to-day existence, moving from one crisis to another and hoping things will somehow work out in the end. Leaders in the Body of Christ are to set the pace for ministry, and be active, rather than reactive; "pro-active." That is, with God's help, a leader should plan and program the future, rather than allow the future to plan and program ones life. The lack of growth, financial pressures, personality conflicts, difficulties within the family life, and many other things, can enter into the day-to-day existence of a leader. The end result can lead to burn-out, resignation, or even worse, premature death. Therefore pastors must have a clear direction for the management of time. The following are significant keys to time management that will help a leader to move into full-time pastoral ministry.

First is the whole process of planning. A pastors overall plan for ministry should contain a long-range plan, a mid-range plan, and a short-range plan. The short-range plan is a one-to-three year plan, setting goals for that period of time. The mid-range covers from five to ten years, and the long-range from ten to fifteen years. Begin your planning with the long-range plans first, and then backward-plan to tomorrow.

For instance, as a leader you spend time in prayer and with the family, the Lord may place on your heart the desire to plant a new church, or to see the church being presently pastored grow to a certain number, or perhaps to be involved in some form of international ministry, writing, or other form of speaking or communication. These long-range goals would fit into a ten-to-fifteen year plan. If the leader is thirty years old, they may want to ask, "Where am I going to be when I am forty-five?" and then determine, "What would I like to be doing when I get to that place?" Of course, circumstances can change; that is why nothing is set in concrete. But without a vision for the future, the pastor is likely to end up anywhere. Secondly, the leader would review the goals for a five-to-ten year plan. "Where do I hope to be in terms of my intermediate goals before I reach the long-range goals?" "What steps do I have to accomplish in order to reach the long-term goal?" Perhaps a goal will be to increase ones education or achieve some specialized training, or to make specific contacts. Whatever they are, write them down plainly, so that everyone understands. Following that, a leader will develop one-to-three year goals. As the plan for ones goals develops, it is important to plan in every major area of life, including spiritually. Where would you like to be in terms of spiritual leadership and your relationship with God? In the financial, social, physical health, and vocational arenas, where do you hope to be? As a spiritual leader develops plans, they will find that everything else in ministry prioritization begins to follow.

The process of organizing ones time in the short run follows; monthly meetings, support staff meetings, the preaching calendar, etc. About ninety days prior to the start of a new year is the time to actually calendar out the entire activities for the coming year. This is usually done with the help of family, friends, presbytery, elders, and deacons. They all give their varied input to the overall church calendar. Lay out as much as a year or more in advance, events that will be important in the life of the church.

Some have criticized this method, fearing that it will stifle the move of the Holy Spirit. Yet if anything, it enhances the movement of the Holy Spirit in the church. It also helps the leader to know, for prayer and planning purposes, what is likely to occur at any given time during the year. It provides for significant stability for the entire church.

Of course, as a calendar develops, make sure that someone attends to the calendar to avoid conflicts in overall church planning and purposes. From the annual calendar one will want to make a monthly calendar, a weekly calendar, including staff meetings, counseling times, etc., and eventually the daily calendar.

A final word regarding time management seems appropriate here. Every good leader must learn to delegate both their authority and their responsibility to subordinates that work with them. These subordinates can be either paid staff, which is very rare for a first pastorate, or volunteer staff, more likely the case. Remember that most volunteers are highly committed to the cause of Christ, and yet are often busy people trying to do their best to function in their world. Therefore use diplomacy when delegating authority and responsibility.

Leaders must delegate more authority than responsibility because the buck stops with the senior man or woman in charge of a ministry or business. Thus, though pastors delegate responsibility, the leader must also delegate the authority and resources to assist that individual to effectively fulfill what they have been tasked with. One of the greatest difficulties that pastors have is, not in asking people to help, but in actually allowing them to help in their own style, rather than exactly as the pastor would have them do it. Trust people enough to allow them to succeed or fail, to let them function in a way that makes sense to them. How the job is done is often less important than actually accomplishing the task, as long as the process is an ethical one. Delegation is vitally important. It maximizes ones time by allowing others to share the burden. God has not called leaders to be messiahs carrying every burden of the church. He has called shepherds to lead and to feed. Thus leaders must allow others to share in the load in an effective and an appropriate manner.

Time management is by far one of the most difficult things for most pastors to do. It is perfectly acceptable to ask for help if needed. Make sure that the personal calendar balances all the things required, especially rest and relaxation. Ultimately, God wants His pastors to function in ministry for the long haul, to see the fulfillment of the destiny God has preordained for ministering effectively into ones sixty's, seventy's, and beyond if the Lord should tarry.

THOUGHT QUESTIONS

1. What are long-range, mid-range, and short-range goals?
2. Describe how you will set your plans.
3. What is an important daily step to not overlook in carrying out one's plans?
4. List up to 8 dangers of not adequately prioritizing one's time.
5. Does planning stifle the move of the Holy Spirit? Why or why not?

SECTION II:
THE LEADER IN LEADERSHIP

CHAPTER 8
THE LEADER AS FATHER/SERVANT-LEADER

"Know well the condition of your flocks, and pay attention to your herds. For riches are not forever, nor does a crown endure to all generations. When the grass disappears, the new growth is seen, and the herbs of the mountains are gathered in, the lambs will be for your clothing, and the goats will bring the price of a field, and there will be goat's milk enough for your food, for the food of your household, and sustenance for your maidens," **(Proverbs 27:23-27 NAS).**

Everyone has a flock, whether a parent overseeing a family, a business man overseeing personnel, policy, and procedures within a business, or a pastor tending the affairs of the church. Each leader has a flock, people to whose care they are committed. One of the greatest cries within churches today is to find pastoral or apostolic leadership that flows from a father's heart, the heart of a Servant-Leader. Young men and women are looking for strong biblical models. They look for those who are willing to sacrifice their own personal desires and needs to care for them, and show them how to become a father, or mother, of the faith. People need pastors who are strong, mature, and able to effectively care for their flocks.

In this passage of scripture, the Word of God speaks of characteristics necessary to show proper care for the flock of God. One of the primary words in this passage is the Hebrew word *charuwts*, or diligence. To know well the condition of one's flock is to be diligent, to watch over it with due diligence. The word *diligence* means a threshing sledge having sharp teeth, gold as mined, a trench as dug. Or it means determination, to be eager, decisive, and incisive.

The Word of God talks much about diligence. Proverbs

21:5 states,

> *"The plans of the diligent lead surely to advantage, but everyone who is hasty comes surely to poverty."*

In Proverbs 12:24 we read,

> *"The hand of the diligent will rule but the slack hand will be put to forced labor."*

Proverbs 13:4 warns,

> *"The soul of the sluggard craves, and gets nothing. But the soul of the diligent is made fat."*

Another relevant passage is Proverbs 10:4,

> *"Poor is he who works with a negligent hand, but the hand of the diligent makes rich."*

The New Testament also places an emphasis on diligence in ministry.

> *"Now for this very reason also, applying all diligence, in your faith, supply moral excellence and in your moral excellence, knowledge.... Therefore brethren, be all the more diligent to make certain about his calling and choosing you, for as long as you practice these things, [that which was talked about above] you will never stumble,"* **(II Peter 1:5, 10 NAS).**

The Apostle Peter writes to the church at large, and especially to the leadership of the church of his day. His emphasis on the need for diligence cannot be over emphasized.

A final passage that speaks very strongly to the importance of diligence is Rom. 12:8,

> *"He who exhorts, in his exhortation, He who gives, with liberality, and he who leads, with diligence, and he who shows mercy, with cheerfulness."*

Leaders in the house of God must lead with diligence.

Attention is another word used in the scripture to described the importance of knowing and properly caring for your flock. Leaders, and people in general, attend to whatever or whomever they really love. Therefore, as leaders, ones heart should be focused in the same direction and on the same things as God.

> *"Take heed, keep on the alert; for you do not know when the appointed time is. It is like a man away on a journey, who upon leaving his house and putting his slaves in charge, assigning to each one his task, also commanded the doorkeeper to stay on the alert. Therefore, be on the alert [or pay close attention]—for you do not know when the master of the house is coming, whether in the evening, at midnight, at cock-crowing, or in the morning—lest He come suddenly and find you asleep. What I say to you I say to all, 'Be on the alert,'"* **(Mark 13:33-37 NAS)**

Hebrews 13:17 states,

> *"Obey your leaders, and submit to them, for they keep watch over your souls as those who will give an account. Let them do this with joy and not with grief, for this would be unprofitable to you."*

Giving proper oversight is part of the responsibility of spiritual leaders. The father-heart of a pastor ensures that the young are well cared for, so that they might mature to become all that God created them to be.

The Proverbs 27 passage also advises shepherds to be careful about priorities. The ministry should never be a source of personal engrandizement or of riches. God cares that His leaders be diligently obedient to God's Word, focusing on the fulfillment of Jesus' prayer in John 17:22,

> *"That they all might be one, as the Father and Son are one."*

Remember also Mat. 6:33,

> *"Seek first the Kingdom of God and His righteousness, and all these things shall be added unto you."*

The church looks at the pastor as a father who sets forth the priority for the church. Are they true servant-leaders? Do they care for the things of God first, the people of God second, and finally care for their own needs? Or do they focus primarily on building a comfortable living off of the work that they do in the Kingdom of God? There is a balance. God will make adequate provision for His called and anointed leaders from the work of ones hands. This is promised to Gods leaders as seen in Proverbs 27 and Matthew 6:33. when proper, diligent care in the house of God. is shown, profit will follow. Diligent care for the flock of God, paying proper attention to the needs of God's house, will lead to success in the purpose of God.

> *"I solemnly charge you in the presence of God and of Jesus Christ, who is to judge the living and the dead, and by His appearing and His Kingdom, preach the Word; be ready in season and out of*

season; reprove, rebuke, exhort, with great patience and instruction. For the time will come when they will not endure sound doctrine but wanting to have their ears tickled, they will accumulate for themselves teachers in accordance to their own desires. And will turn away their ears from the truth and will turn aside to myths. but you be sober in all things, endure hardships, do the work of an evangelist, fulfill your ministry," **(II Tim. 4:1-5)**

God charges pastors to fulfill their ministry, whatever that ministry call is. In order to do that, leaders must focus upon diligence in every aspect of their walk with God. The servant-leader shepherding the flock of God *will* see the fruit of their labor.

THE PASTOR AS SEEN BY THE PEOPLE

People in the general congregation see many different things when they look at the man or woman of God standing in the pulpit. Some see simply a preacher who has an inordinate desire and need to proclaim the good news of Jesus Christ and to instruct people in a public forum. They see you as a public speaker. Others see the ideal person, friend, companion, husband, and father. People inevitably see these roles in the life and the ministry of a pastor.

Very little can be done about them other than to clarify the reality: that all of us have been called to be servant-leaders in the Body of Christ regardless of our specific office of Five-Fold ministry calling. Leaders stand as servants of the Most High God with a specific calling to minister the grace and mercy of God to God's wonderful people.

Our calling by God to servant-leadership is best seen in the role of a father. People often see and attempt to relate, positively or negatively, to the pastor in his role as father. As children see their natural fathers, so people tend to view their spiritual father, the local church leader. Of course, this places a distinct responsibility upon the shoulders of that leader. As has been already discussed, the pastor stands in abstencia for God Himself. People look to the spiritual leader as a representative of God, whether or not that role perception is wanted. Every leader knows only too well their weaknesses of the flesh and character. How fallible is the man and woman of God, who as with any other human being has their own hang-ups, problems and needs. But the congregation rarely knows, or even considers, such things. Pastors are truly like parents to them. As such, rather than denying the reality of the power of this role, leaders must flow with the anointing and power that God has given us, with the authority of the Word as leaders in the Body of Christ, to assist people to come to maturity in God.

Spiritual leaders are in a position to be healing agents for many who have had broken relationships from times past. Many have been blessed with a wonderful father figure. Too often, however, people have had a problematic relationship with their father. He has either been absent, or presented an inconsistent father figure. These people will often have difficulty relating to God as Father because of the lack of a father figure in their life. Spiritual leaders have the unique opportunity to manifest or exhibit the characteristics of God's loving fatherhood to His children through preaching, teaching and role-modeling within the Body of Christ. Sensitive leaders can set in motion the healing power of God for people in the local church.

It would be helpful, then, to look at the godly role of father and some of the attributes of a fathering figure, which is certainly what leaders are within the Body of Christ.

THE FATHER ROLE

One of the most profound statements that can be found in the Word of God regarding God in His role as father is found in Ps. 68:5.

"A father of the fatherless, and a judge for the

*widows, is God in His holy habitation," * **(KJV).**

Further, Isa. 64:8 states,

"But now, O LORD, thou art our Father; we are the clay, and thou our Potter; and we all are the work of Thy hand" **(KJV).**

The fatherhood of God can be seen in all creation. God created everything good. When He created mankind, He proclaimed it to be very good. One can see the very craftsmanship of God in each individual life from the child to the great-grandparent. The love of God in the care he gives to all of creation, and especially to man, is awe-inspiring. The Word of God indicates that He has a special heart of love for those who are widows and orphans, those who have had less advantaged lives. Truly, a father's heart is a heart for the oppressed, the suffering, and those who have endured special losses of the loved and cherished. As leaders, our hearts should be a servant-leader's heart, hearts of caring for those that are less fortunate in the Body of Christ.

Leaders very lives should be in intimate connectedness with the Father. In Matthew 6:9 we read;

"Pray then in this way; Our Father who are in heaven, hallowed be Thy name," **(KJV).**

Further, Matt. 7:11 says,

"If you being evil know how to give good gifts to your children, how much more shall your father which is in heaven give what is good to those that ask him?"

A good and loving father is approachable, and will listen with compassion. The business of ministerial life can rob pastors of the most vital human resource. If one does not take time for those less significant or for those whose tithe is limited, the opportunity to act as our Father acts can be missed. Father-God is more than ready, willing to listen with intimate compassion to the needs of His children. Not only is He willing to listen, He is willing to give that which He has to give. Human pastors, of course, can give only so much. There is only so much time and resource available. Whatever God has given, and is available to give, whatever good one can do, should flow from a heart of love to God's wonderful children.

Perhaps the best picture of a father's love can be found in Rom. 8:15:

> *"For you have not received a spirit of slavery leading to fear, but you have received a spirit of adoption as sons by which we cry out, Abba Father."*

Daddy Father. God truly is a daddy, a loving father who has chosen His children above all others to be members of his family.

Historically, when a citizen of the Roman-occupied kingdom chose to adopt a child, the adoption ceremony was public, regardless of the age of the child. The child was brought into a strategic area where all the people could see the procedure. The child was then placed on the lap of the father. As the father held that child, everyone present recognized that regardless of this child's origins, history, or difficulties, the past was ancient history. Before the ceremony concluded, the child was given a new name representing his completely transformed identity. He was now a citizen of the kingdom and a member of this new household.

When God adopts a person through Christ into the Family, they are treated as royalty, as princes and princesses in the kingdom of God. As leaders of a flock of the people of God, ones heart should exhibit a similar flavor. A pastors desire should be to lift the people of God in their own eyes, to lift them from past inadequate perceptions, releasing them to a recognition of their new image: new creations in Christ. They are truly new citizens. Oh, they are still under tutelage, not knowing everything yet, and discipleship must occur, including discipline and correction. But regardless, they are members of the kingdom of God to be treated with honor and great respect.

As pastors in a father's role, great responsibility is given for the care and feeding of the sheep of God. Leaders feed and lead, caring for them in times of difficulty. As role models, leaders portray the reality that our loving God in heaven will consistently be there for them through good times and bad. Role models in the natural are far from perfect. No spiritual leader can be all places at all times. Yet by God's power and grace, leaders are empowered to raise up others to assist in the glorious work of the Kingdom of God. These helpers will also be father figures; elders, deacons, and those in specific ministries, who will be able to provide the grace and mercy of God to those in need.

THOUGHT QUESTIONS

1. List 2 characteristics necessary to show proper care for the flock of God.
2. As servant-leaders, how do we find the power to continually give?
3. The Father is our model for leadership and service. List some of His attributes that we should emulate.
4. As role models imitating the Father, what do we want the sheep to learn about God?

Chapter 9
The Leader as Administrator

As we continue in this section on The Pastor in Leadership, there are several other vitally important pastoral roles or functions for every pastor or spiritual leader. The first is by far the most problematic for many pastors, even more than that of counselor; the role of pastor as administrator.

In actuality, most pastors are many things; CEO of a corporation, primary teacher and spiritual mentor, counselor, priest, and healer. All of those functions are historically given to the local pastor. But being an administrator is usually the most problematic for pastors, being the organizer of a hopefully growing local ministry. This section will address very clearly the role of the pastor as administrator, and provide some specific helps.

One of the most difficult areas of ministry, as expressed by most spiritual leaders, is that of administration. It *does* seem as though the paperwork never ends! Between government reporting, reports to the congregation, and the letters and faxes that must be generated on a regular basis, it is very easy for men and women in spiritual oversight to become bogged down in the day-to-day minutiae of paper. Yet one need not be defeated by the paperwork of life. There really isn't a paperwork demon; it just seems that way. As in every area of life, God wants for His leaders to be as professional as possible, so as to overcome the obstacles to administrative management of a local church.

This chapter reviews in limited detail various aspects of administration, from a principle viewpoint or a conceptual vantage point, as well as examining practicalities of overall church administration and organization. Hopefully, this introduction to this vast area will pique a pastors interest in conducting more study regarding church administration. First, it is important to observe some basic principles for overall church or ministry organization.

PLANNING FOR GROWTH

When dialoging about church administration, the topic being addressed is the actual planning for church or ministry growth. When planning for growth, keep in mind the biblical description of a New Testament church. A solid theology is essential. An exhaustive study on this important topic cannot be tackled in the context of this volume. This will be the subject of a future book should the Lord allow.

True growth will take place within any church fellowship if several demands are met. Growth demands change. Change is frightening. Most people prefer things to remain just the way they have always been. If pastors are going to see growth occur, they must be willing to make changes which are sometimes organizational, sometimes programmatic, and sometimes in terms of overall planning.

Growth demands sharing the workload. If growth is to occur in a systematic fashion, the leadership must have help. The apostles certainly discovered this.

> *Now at this time while the disciples were increasing in number, a complaint arose on the part of the Hellenistic Jews against the native Hebrews, because their widows were being overlooked in the daily serving of food. And the twelve summoned the congregation of the disciples and said, "It is not desirable for us to neglect the word of God in order to serve tables. But select from among you, brethren, seven men of good reputation, full of the Spirit and of wisdom, whom we may put in charge of this task. But we will devote ourselves to prayer, and to the ministry of the word." And the statement found approval with the whole congregation; and they chose Stephen, a man full of faith and of the Holy Spirit, and Philip, Prochorus, Nicanor, Timon, Parmenas and*

Nicolas, a proselyte from Antioch. And these they brought before the apostles: and after praying, they laid their hands on them," **(Acts 6:1-6 NAS).**

If the Apostles would have attempted to fill all the needs of the first-century church single-handedly, they would have certainly burned out. In order to accomplish the distribution of the food to the Hellenistic Jews, the Apostles recognized that it was essential to find men and women who were already actively involved in servanthood ministry, with proven gifts and capabilities to marshal the task. These helpers, all of which were Hellenistic Jews as well as removing the fear of favoritism), were filled with the dynamic power of the Holy Spirit, and were able to serve the people adequately. The apostles were then able to carry on with the work to which God had primarily called them: prayer and the ministry of the Word of God. Leaders must be willing and able to delegate ones authority and the responsibility for certain aspects of the workload. Thus, more can be done, and more people will be utilized for Kingdom business. The more committed people are to the work of God, and the more active they are in accomplishing tasks that lead to the fulfillment of the overall vision for the church, the happier they will be.

Sharing the workload can be difficult for many pastors, especially if they are somewhat impulsive and highly motivated to see quick results. Yet a pastors' greatest results are gained by sharing the workload and motivating people to participate in the work of the local church.

Growth demands a plan. Without an action plan, pastors essentially plan to fail. Any plan should begin with the vision of the local church, given to the leadership hopefully by the Holy Spirit, and the mission or the purpose of that specific assembly within a local community. The mission statement should be clearly spelled out. Following that should be basic objectives and goals, and then plans to fulfill those goals and objectives. These plans are woven into the overall function of the local church and are a part of the general job descriptions of people who are actively involved in the work of the church. Thus, everything works more smoothly, accountability systems are established, and distribution of work becomes much easier.

Growth demands that people learn to work together in unity. If two walk the same road, they *must* be in agreement (Amos 3:3). Not only does this include the senior pastor and whatever associate staff he or she may have, but it also involves all who are active in *any* area of leadership.

Someone must be in charge. God has determined that the pastor, and secondarily the elders who have been raised up in a local fellowship, are the primary leaders in a church. Further, in most cities there are other "watchmen" who can serve in an advisory presbytery, giving oversight and input to the local pastor and elders. No church should be led by the Sunday School teacher, for example, or by the janitor. Their jobs and functions are important, and in many cases, vital, especially on a Sunday morning if the toilet has suddenly overflowed. The major decisions and direction for the local church must flow from those called of God into that place of leadership, and qualified to be in that position.

The rest of the leadership in a local fellowship must be willing to humbly submit to the leadership over them and work together for a common good.

Finally, growth demands dedication. There is no endeavor in life, whether business, politics, or church life, where *perspiration* is not the most important element in terms of activity. Leaders need men and women in the church who are fully dedicated to the task of church growth. Growth means more than just numbers. It also includes the deepening of spiritual virtue (righteousness) in the people of God and strength for those involved in the local assembly.

There are always demands placed upon local pastors to see growth occur. Growth will occur, in the timing of the Lord, as the pastor and other oversight joyously pursue the demands of growth with a heart filled with expectation. God is more interested in growing the church than the most committed of spiritual leaders.

MANAGEMENT

Certain principles of management must be followed to ensure that the plans and procedures that have been outlined by the leadership are actually accomplished. Management is the development of people, not just the direction of "things." The Word of God speaks about the need to build into the lives of people skills necessary for them to lead others to the fullness of Christ. This is pictured in Ex. 18, in the advice given by Jethro to Moses. Jethro gave good advice, but was the advice actually God-given? Jethro may have been quite correct that Moses might burn himself out if he continued at the pace he was moving. The advice to raise up leaders to assist in sharing the load in many ways was good, but many of those leaders later became a thorn in the flesh for dear brother Moses.

In the book of Numbers, Moses complained to God about his heavy load and cried out for help. God brought seventy elders who were already full of His Spirit who could come along side Moses and assist him in the organization and management of the children of Israel. There are often good ideas, and then there may be ***God-ideas***. As leaders, the pursuit of God ideas, often found in the prayer closet and born of adversity are the ideas which will bring eternal results.

In practical terms, the principle of management should flow with the management of people. Pastors should be willing to look for faithful men and faithful women into whom they can impart their life and vision. These faithful people will be willing to take positions of leadership and contribute to the work. They need to be members of the local church, willing to follow the leader, and selected by the leaders of that local assembly. The selection of leaders should never be taken lightly. Christ prayed all night before selecting His followers (Luke 6:12-13). Also note that Jesus selected twelve from amongst many that had initially followed Him. It is unclear from the scriptures how Jesus made the selections, but they were made in consultation and agreement with the Father. Also, the advisory presbytery can be a true blessing in the selection of primary leaders for a local fellowship.

The leaders must be willing to give clear-cut duties and responsibilities to these management or government personnel. These leaders will need supervision, training and assistance, and be given the supplies and tools necessary to fulfill their job, whatever it may be.

Any questions or concerns regarding duties or the authority to act should be resolved quickly and become a part of overall policy.

As pastors manage people, they must recognize that their management should be primarily people-oriented, and secondarily project-oriented. If leaders manage people well, inspiring them to work hard for the Kingdom of God, the projects and a positive outcome of project development will follow.

Why must a pastor be involved in administration at all? The fact is, many requirements must be met in the role of pastor, both from a legal viewpoint, as well as ensuring positive communication to those to whom the pastor is ministering. Ultimately, all administration should flow from the office of the pastor who is clearly called as a member of the Five-Fold ministry, and who recognizes his or her primary function as a member in the Body of Christ.

The focus of administration is to prepare, train and equip the saints of God to do the work of ministry. Administration itself is one area of ministry that must be done. Most pastors can solve their problems with relative speed if they will find and empower someone trainable in administrative functions. According to the Word of God, the pastor cannot do everything himself. He must be willing to delegate to others so that the overall administration of church life may be completed.

To define the term, an administrator is an individual who executes, manages, directs, dispenses, or distributes whatever it is that needs to be done; the act of directing. Three primary patterns of leadership or directing style among executives have been identified. These are called the Dominator, the Compromiser, and the Harmonizer. They are also known as the *autocratic, laissez-*

faire, and the ***democratic*** styles.

The Dominator sees themselves and functions as a relatively blunt, no-nonsense leader. They tend to make decisions for everyone under them. They are very strong advocates of a company, "teamwork" style, but tend to tolerate disagreements with disdain. They believe that participation in management simply means to agree with the decisions *he or she* has already made. Essentially, they believe in a "put up or shut-up" form of leadership. Compromise creates great difficulty. Thus, they carry the basic belief that a strong leader must be an individual that functions from a place of absolute authority and requires obedience in virtually everything. Finally, they tend to rule by intimidation, not by relationship. If mistakes are made, punishment falls quickly and severely.

Many leaders in local churches fit well within this model of management. They are often effective, especially in inner city areas where the ability to make decisions and to discipline, are limited. Unfortunately, the churches under them tend to disintegrate when they depart, unless another leader, not always as benevolent, comes to the fore.

The Compromiser is a relatively easy leader under which to work, especially in comparison to the Dominator. They do not want to push people around because they disagree philosophically with that approach. They look for good results by finding a way to work together in areas of harmony and agreement. They will avoid conflict at any cost. They want to get the job done, but they also wants people to be pleased and happy. they tend towards the pragmatic in overall management orientation, simply looking for various ways to get the job done. Further, the Compromiser will often overlook mistakes, and will rarely discipline even where correction is needed. A high priority for the Compromiser is making peace, but sometimes their peacemaking comes at too high a cost.

The Harmonizer also believes strongly in teamwork. As a leader, they believe that one should be considerate of others, and show understanding to each others' personal needs and desires. At the same time, they strive very hard toward excellence in productivity. The Harmonizer wants to find people who will be compatible to one another and who will have genuine concern for the needs of the members of the Body of Christ. Ultimately, they would like to create an environment where people enjoy participating and working together, especially for the cause of Christ, building mutual trust and confidence in one another.

Each type of leader has strengths and weaknesses. Some of each of these three styles may influence a leader, but one style will tend to dominate. Each style has its place of effectiveness, but for the long run, the Harmonizer tends to be the most effective in their role as pastoral leader.

ORGANIZATION

Regardless of the administrative gifts or leadership style of an individual spiritual overseer, leadership and management require organization. Pastors often organize the local church according to patterns, which have already been learned, some of which may be quite healthy and effective. As discussed previously, a leaders must be willing to change if growth is to occur. Organization became essential in many places in the Word of God to ensure the completion of a task. Jesus organized the Twelve before sending them out two by two. A significant amount of organization was required for the feeding of the five thousand. Organization is seen in the selection of the seven deacons and in the development of the local church. Paul, Barnabas, and Silas raised up elders and deacons in the various churches that they planted, as part of the expansion of the gospel in the first century church.

Organization in the church is essential in order to reach the largest number of people with the gospel. People need to accomplish meaningful work; not just busy work, but that which furthers the goals and vision of the local church. Organization is needed for the purposes of coordination, direction and continuity of church life, including cooperation with other churches in order to see a greater good occur within a community.

Proper organization prevents the overlapping and overlooking of needs within a congregation. The apostles in Acts 6 were clearly unaware that the food distribution was not going as smoothly as they hoped. Thus it came to their attention, and they took action. With proper organization in place, leaders are able to anticipate and give oversight *before* the needs occurring within the Body of Christ are overlooked.

Dr. Albert Beavens[1] provides five elements of effective organization: They are (with personal commentary):

1. Clearly see the task to be accomplished.
2. Be willing to select, enlist, and prepare leaders who are able and wise enough to lead in a successful accomplishment of the task.
3. Help these leaders to see the task and inspire them to do it. As a part of that, one will hopefully show others the big picture and how their part fits into the overall accomplishment of the vision for the church.
4. Place the load of the accomplishment of the given task squarely on their shoulders, and require that they carry out their responsibility fully and adequately. Leaders should provide for accountability. Amazingly, pastors will often delegate a task but never check to see if it was finished. When an individual does not finish and is never brought to accountability, he learns that the pastor's wishes do not really matter. They are rarely willing to volunteer to work for the church again.
5. Provide inspiration for their efforts by counsel and friendship. Show each group and its leaders how their work relates to the total work of the local church. All efforts should lead back to the overall vision.

---

[1] *The Local Church, Its Purpose and Program.* New York, Abbington Press, 1937, pg. 166.

Thus, part of the role of a local church pastor or elder in leadership is to keep their eyes open for any who demonstrates leadership ability. That leadership ability is extremely important. When someone is found with the remotest ability, they need to be drawn into leaderships confidence, find their areas of interest, and begin to train and equip them to take responsibility that will lead to the blessing of others within the Body of Christ.

The primary tasks of oversight, which is likely to engage every administrator, i.e., senior pastor, can be broken down into three broad categories. The first are the spiritual activities of the church. These include the overall organization and administration of the worship services, such as:

- Who is to preach, lead worship, etc.
- Any evangelistic or other special services.
- Prayer and praise services.
- Specialized services such as baptism or the Lord's Supper.
- Wedding and funeral services.
- Special dedications.
- Ordinations, as God raises up leaders within your church. These are the primary spiritual activities. More will be discussed on these areas, and the programs of ministry for a local church leader, in later chapters. Secondly, the overseer, usually the pastor or church administrator, oversees the business matters of the church, including but not limited to:
- The tasks and activities of the elder or trustee board.
- Oversight of the upkeep of the church property. That does not mean that the pastor must personally clean the toilets and paint the walls, although when first starting out, they very well may. Rather, the Pastor will supervise or oversee, to ensure that the needs are properly cared for.

- Protection of the flock and God's resources.
- Other various needs, such as insurance, etc.
- Preparing and raising the church budget. This includes oversight of all the finances within the local church.
- Oversight, for special purposes, of new church construction, improvement, and/or enlargement of present facilities.
- Oversight of church accounting and record keeping systems which are required by law.
- Proper communication within the local church.
- Oversight of the business meetings of the church, including the annual reports provided to the entire congregation.

The responsibilities listed in this second section are usually the least exciting for most pastors. However, if done well, it will create less difficulty in areas of *spiritual* service within the local church.

Third and often neglected, a church administrator or pastoral leader is responsible to administer the general program for the development of a healthy tone of interpersonal relationships with the people of God. A shepherd is responsible to provide an atmosphere whereby people can express their feelings, needs and hurts, in a positive, caring atmosphere. Thus, the spiritual leader must familiarize themselves with various forms of communication, written and oral, to be able to facilitate this task.

Along with being concerned about these primary organizational areas, keep in mind the primary goals for all churches regarding their active involvement's. First and foremost, all churches should be involved in New Testament evangelism. The primary program for evangelism and revival is that of church planting. Every church should be involved in planting other churches, thus expanding the Kingdom of God. Second is to provide for Christian care, including healing and restoration of those that are broken. Further, pastors need to be actively involved in the strengthening of families. Any time that homes are strengthened, the local church and community are strengthened. Thus a family orientation is vital for the building of a local fellowship. Fourth, senior leadership should be community-involved. A local fellowship can best serve a community for its' betterment by active involvement in community activity. This should include outreach for the poor, ministry to widows and orphans, etc. Fifth, pastors and leaders in general should be friendly, open and warm, both in the church and in the community. Sixth, an international missions mandate is needed to keep the local church from being too myopic. Any church that neglects missions becomes self-absorbed, and will miss much of the reason for existence. They only see themselves, limiting their ability to influence others. Finally, leaders need to exhibit concern for the whole Body of Christ, and its strength.

From these various goals, leadership will develop plans to obtain them. They include such things as the building of the local church, leading and worship, preaching the gospel, teaching God's people, being willing to do pastoral care and counseling, praying, planting, and developing programs that will meet the specific needs of a local community. All of these are a part of the organizational tasks that leaders must be willing to tackle as growth in a local fellowship occurs. Growth comes through overall administration. Administration comes through departmentalization. Departmentalization of local churches is needed in order to properly grow on a wider foundation. Anticipating growth and the organization for growth must occur *before* the need for growth occurs. Remember that as leaders organize, it is done with a focus towards the future, building on a larger or wider foundation to ensure that the needs of a local community are met.

THOUGHT QUESTIONS
1. List some demands that must be met in order to realize growth.
2. What is management's orientation?
3. Which style of management is most effective, and why?
4. What does management focus on, and why?
5. Church growth does not only refer to numbers. To what else does it refer?
6. List the 5 elements of effective organization as outlined by Dr. Beavens.

CHAPTER 10
THE LEADER AND PROGRAMS
WHAT IS PLANNING?

According to Webster, a plan is *"a method or scheme of procedure or arrangement, a project, program, outline, or schedule."*

Church planning is the outlining of a total strategy for accomplishing the stated objectives of the local church. The plan should flow from the overall vision for that church and its mission statement. This planning can take two primary forms; long-range planning which is usually a projection of from two to five years, and short range planning, which includes the program for a year, broken down into specific goals, with backward planning to the day that implementation begins.

Why should pastors plan the local church? Shouldn't leaders be, especially as Charismatic or Pentecostal believers, fully open to the flow of the Holy Spirit, simply doing whatever God wants? Of course, pastors *do* want to do what God wants and allow for the Holy Spirit to flow. But everything that God has done, He has done within a framework of organization and control. Even the universe follows certain established laws that have been instituted by God. Churches also need to run according to godly principles, including the principle of planning.

Planning enables the staff, workers and individual members of the local church to anticipate what is likely to occur during any specific time frame. It also relates the various parts of the local church to its whole, which is vitally important. It also enables a person to more clearly grasp the purpose of the church's existence. Although the leadership may be very clear as to what God has called the church to, the rest of the church may not be so clear. Thus it is inherent upon God's leaders to provide a clear rationale in thorough planning and program development, so the church will know in *what* they are involved, and *why*.

Planning assists the church in knowing at what stage they

are and where they are headed. Thus they will be able to check and chart their progress. Planning provides a systematic approach to the implementing of the church's objectives. It allows for evaluating its progress to ensure sharper focus for future development. Planning avoids unnecessary waste in activity and finances, by unifying and correlating the activities and functions of the local church. Planning develops creativity, in terms of what and how the work of God is accomplished.

There are several things that must be decided in the development overall planning. It begins with the question of who does what? The overall focus of planning must flow first from the senior pastor, and then from those that are designated leadership. That leadership includes every department leader, such as the Sunday School chairman or director, outreach ministry director, Worship leader, as well as those involved in other areas of leadership, such as the elders and deacons. Everyone that has a vested interest in the development of the local church should be a part of their organizational structure, especially in planning and procedures.

Secondly, how is it to be done? Keep in mind certain helpful thoughts. First, planning should flow from a logical process rather than helter-skelter. It should develop realistic objectives and goals as part of the overall planning. Planning must be inclusive, involving the total church program for that specific fiscal or calendar year. Flexibility should accompany planning. The plan is simply a means to an end, not the end in itself.

Planning must be projected into the future, for continuity and direction. It is very helpful to start your future planning by having a meeting with the entire leadership. It is helpful to meet several weeks or months ahead of the implementation of the plan, to set time aside for prayer and such functions as brainstorming.

You, the overall spiritual leader, will be presenting to the planning meeting a general guideline of what the church is about. You will also present before the people the overall vision. If the vision is to reach the community for Christ, you should state that clearly. If your vision is to build a family oriented local church, state that clearly. Vision statements are often a brief picture taken from the Word of God, with your specific emphasis, which illustrates the thrust of your local fellowship. From the vision you will develop a mission statement. What are we going to do as we go about fulfilling the vision? Then, based upon the various needs of your congregation, you will develop objectives for each department that will flow toward the fulfillment of the overall vision and mission statement.

For example, in the Christian Education department, you may have an objective of increasing the number of children within the Sunday School Department by ten percent over the next year. If you have fifty people in your Sunday School program, a ten percent increase would be five additional people, an extremely modest and obtainable objective. You may wish to increase it significantly. Or you may state an objective to build a solid Sunday School program to meet the needs of your local church. The goals might include: 1) Find teachers, determining the number needed. 2) We must bring more children into the program, increased by X amount. Then you develop your plan for that department. How are we going to go about meeting the goal and the objective for this department? All of that, then, goes into an overall document of which everyone within the local church needs to be aware.

The overall planning calendar for the church for that year will follow the outline of various departmental needs. If one of the goals is to build a Sunday School, we may need to have a Sunday School campaign or two during the year. Those campaigns would be programmed into the calendar at a time when everyone can help give support to the program. If an objective for the ministry is to develop a nursing home outreach, emphasis for that ministry should be provided during the year. Thus, as you develop your overall calendar, everything will flow together.

In the back of this textbook, you will find for your information a sample annual calendar developed by a dynamic local church in Brooklyn, New York, Bay Ridge Christian Center. It is used here with their permission. It is a good sample model that you can use for your planning purposes.

Once plans are developed, they must be coordinated with the one who will oversee the general church calendar to ascertain that all is flowing without conflict. As the planning process concludes, the entire plan is presented to the congregation. Charts or other forms of communication are helpful to show everyone in the local church the comprehensive plans, so they can prayerfully involve themselves in what God is doing in the congregation.

HOW TO MOTIVATE PEOPLE TO SERVE

The greatest complaint that I hear from pastors, beyond the overall administrative burden of the church, is in the *motivation* of God's people to work within the church. How does one motivate an individual, essentially a volunteer, to serve?

At best, fifteen to twenty percent of the local congregation accomplishes eighty percent of the work. This has been true in evangelical churches for as long as statistics have been kept, an unfortunate reality. Churches that are truly growing in the Kingdom of God have been able to break through this twenty percent barrier. They have significantly more of the congregation actively involved in the ministry.

Why are some people in the congregation unwilling to serve?

First, the average layman is unclear about two primary things. They are unclear regarding their role in the church, and uncertain about the objectives of the church. Perhaps they do not know that the Holy Spirit has provided spiritual gifts to him or her and through the exercise of these spiritual gifts, they can make a significant contribution to their local church. Remember, the church exists for four purposes: Evangelism, worship, education or training, and fellowship. They are unaware as to how they might fit into one or another area of ministry. They must be educated and motivated by leadership, enlightened as to how they might exercise their unique gifts.

Secondly, the average lay person suffers from a sense of inferiority, especially in light of professional ministry. They do not feel capable or qualified to do much of worth. They need the assurance that they will be equipped, prepared and supported if they move into an area of service.

Finally, the average lay person has never been challenged! Most pastors indicate that if their members merely show up on Sunday, give an offering, or perhaps tithe, that they will be meeting the expectation for a true Christian. What a far cry from the New Testament Church, when the norm was virtually one hundred percent participation and the giving of all that one had! We have come a long way from the apostolic model.

There are some great ways to *squelch or destroy motivation*. They include: Overload. When a capable worker is found, pastors tendency is to pour work on them until they finally break or fall apart. Secondly, the importance people play in terms of their service to the Lord is frequently minimized. Rather than encouraging people and giving public testimony of their importance in the Body of Christ, leaders often either ignore or fail to provide to them the kind of encouragement and affirmation they need. Thirdly, pastors often fail to ensure that the prospective worker will receive the needed materials and training. The concept that lay leaders or perspective leaders should be as highly motivated as the pastor is a misnomer. They should not be allowed to sink or swim based upon their own merits. Given that choice, most will choose not to enter the water at all. If leadership fails to compliment a worker before criticizing him, or tell others in the local church how disappointed they are about his service, this can devastate a worker. Pastors must realize by now that the three fastest forms of communication (short of Internet) is telephone, telefax, and tele-church member! If a leaders wants to start a fire, criticize one member to another, and then see what happens.

Pastoral leaders must be actively involved in motivating people positively by communicating clearly the expectations of a job to be accomplished and continuously affirming their importance to the work of God. In doing so, the people's effectiveness will improve. Further, this positive communication can help to recruit others for much needed assistance. The pastors own involvement, excitement and enthusiasm about what God is doing is contagious! This does not refer to self-inflation or bragging. Others will respond when leaders simply and enthusiastically relate how great and marvelous the Lord is and how wonderful it will be to all work together to see the Kingdom of God expanded.

Some other practical suggestions that can be incorporated to motivate reluctant leaders include:

- Preaching on subjects that deal with the gifts of the Holy Spirit.
- Challenging people to look at their areas of gifting.
- Willingness to spend time with people in the church that show a desire for leadership.
- Helping to draw out of others their various gifts. Once those gifts are determined, it is then inherent upon leadership to begin plugging them into areas where they can exercise their gift effectively. As stated previously, but which cannot be over emphasized, leaders need to be willing to delegate the responsibility and the authority to see jobs accomplished. As delegation occurs, freedom to accomplish tasks in their own style will naturally follow. It is helpful to recognize on a regular basis those that are doing work in the Kingdom of God with such things as certificates of achievement. Tangible rewards are good. The presentation of special little gifts can help build a sense of purpose and meaning. Affirmation is vital and desperately needed, including personal compliments, recognition from the pulpit, and just noticing well-done tasks.

As needs develop, such as in leadership, be willing to announce the need and actively recruit people for involvement in ministry. One pastor has said that he does not believe in volunteers. There should be no such thing as volunteers, since all of us have already volunteered to be members of the Army of God. People need to be challenged and given places of responsibility so that the goals of the overall church can be accomplished.

As in any area of leadership, the pastor, as a servant-leader, has a focus and task of continuously motivating the leaders under him to fulfill the vision of the local church. The ability to motivate people to work in the programs that have been designed and developed by the leadership is very much an art form, and should flow from the desire of the pastor to see excellence throughout all areas of the ministry.

THOUGHT QUESTIONS

1. What does planning accomplish for the church?
2. What contributes to creating the 20% barrier?
3. The church exists for which 4 purposes?
4. How can the leader destroy others' motivation?
5. Name at least 3 positive ways to increase motivation to service.

CHAPTER 11
THE LEADER IN PUBLIC LIFE

Society's image of the pastor has been seriously tarnished over the past few years. The pastoral profession is no longer perceived as one of the most trusted vocations because of public scandal and the cynicism of the western world. Pastors are no longer looked upon as paragons of virtue but are often viewed suspiciously. Perhaps that is why the Apostle Paul in his admonition to the Apostle Timothy stated that we must have a good report of them that are without and within (I Tim. 3:7).

Ones public life should not be inconsistent with ones private life. In fact, both private *and* public life should be circumspect. Pastors should be living a life of godliness, holiness and love. That is certainly the goal, although few fully achieve it. This is not to suggest that a pastor should be perfect, although the concept is comforting. In reality, all leaders are human, subject to areas of weakness. Nevertheless, one should live a life of consistency to the best of ones ability, as God gives strength, before the body of Christ, with ones family, and in the community. Pastors are truly ambassadors for Christ to the community. When people think about the church, its good *or* bad is often linked to the local community pastor. Pastors, are citizens in the community at large in which God has placed them, and are responsible before God, and before others, to live a life of influence; literally to be salt and light in the world.

As the moral standard within a local community, Pastors are asked to speak on moral issues. As they do so, as much as lies within them, partisan politics should be removed from ones speech. Presidents come and go, congressmen fade away, and policies shift with the wind, but the Pastors' stance for righteousness and true holiness should always remain constant.

As a citizen and member of a community, pastors have a fiduciary responsibility for the care of that community. The minister does not just pastor churches, but pastors or elders serve within a locality. People *do* watch pastoral leaders at all times. Because of the special position, pastors are many times exempted from jury duty and military service. They are not compelled to marry people. They are often called upon to dedicate buildings, parks and airports, etc., to speak at graduations and to offer their services at civic functions. As people watch, pastors are ambassadors for Christ and for the local church.

As a public figure, it is helpful to be involved in outside civic activities. Some of those civic activities include the Red Cross or other outreach organizations that are not specifically religious in orientation. When reaching out to the homeless or ministering to the hurting, spiritual leaders show the grace of God in the local community. Graciousness in the community should flow from the pastor, and in serving the community in a non-offensive, clearly Christian manner provides a tremendous witness of the grace of God.

The word of God provides some pictures of the importance of public ministry. Luke 8:1 states:

> ***"Jesus went throughout every city and village preaching and showing the good news of the kingdom of God," (KJV).***

In Acts 20:20, the Apostle Paul states:

> ***"I have taught you publicly, and from house to house," (KJV).***

The ministry of the gospel of Jesus Christ is not to be confined to the walls of the local church. In fact, a tragedy of the West's' edifice-oriented society is that the majority of ministry is done behind closed doors. That was not the way the gospel was initially presented nor the way the local church grew in the New Testament era. In fact, nothing done in the church was secret, but was for the most part proclaimed openly. Everyone understood the Christians' love, outreach and commitment to community.

Therefore it is important even to this day, regardless of the size of the church, to give a certain amount of visitation and visibility to the ministry. Whether the pastor visits church members or provides a setting for public presentation, both are important aspects of ministry.

If one is pastoring a small fellowship, one hundred people or less, including children, the pastor will want to have some sort of a visitation program. This program can include such things as summer barbecues or just visiting members in their homes to give greetings, share heart and vision, or listen to the members concerns. All of this is a form of public ministry.

When the pastor visits church members or local businesses as a religious leader, the leader represents the church or ministry organization they lead. Further, as a representative of Christ to the community it is important to be business-like and professional in manner and conduct.

Pastors are often extremely neglectful of the time, concerns, and constraints of others. Be on time and professional in dealing with people in the community. A positive, prayerful, and practical approach to touching people's lives is very important, whether one is visiting members of the church or local businesses, or becoming involved in civic clubs.

MORE PUBLIC OUTREACH

Other areas of public ministry include the visitation of the sick. Visitation becomes extremely important to many, especially as they reach their latter years of life. They need that special pastoral touch when facing their own eternity. Often, family members do not yet know the Lord. This may be one of the only opportunities the pastor will have to present to this group of lost souls a positive view of the gospel and of Christ's love.

When visiting the sick, call ahead, except for times of emergency. Be prepared to minister faith and hope. Be sympathetic and cheerful in approach to others with the expectation that God will touch them and raise them up.

Proper Ethics

The minister of the gospel has a place of great influence. Therefore, it is important not to prescribe treatment or give medical advice, other than things of good common sense, i.e., to get proper rest, diet, exercise, etc., as long as it is within the individual's ability to perform. Never criticize the treatment prescribed by doctors in front of family members, which may cause great discouragement. If your visitation is to a hospital, one has certain rights as a pastor. The pastor may visit anytime, day or night. A pastor will want to cooperate with the doctors and nurses, because they are (generally) allies in the healing process. When a pastor makes a visitation to a hospital, he or she should not be overly dressed, or under-dressed, nor should they be intrusive. Be cheerful and pleasant in speech, and season with salt ones interactions with the hospital and the patient. When arriving, a pastor should identify themselves without assuming that they will recognize ones position by dress or demeanor.

When visiting one who does not know the Lord, a prime objective is to lead him to Christ. If he is suffering, pray for the alleviation of their suffering. Believe God for healing. It is perfectly appropriate to bring such things as Bible tracts and pictures. Part of the pastors responsibility, many times, is to assist in making family arrangements, especially if the illness is terminal.

A New Child

Another great opportunity for public ministry comes with the birth of a baby. When a mother in the congregation has a child, it is a great opportunity for the pastor to make a positive impact by welcoming this new child into the world. Do not arrive too quickly to the hospital or house after the child is born, but do make oneself visible within a reasonable time frame. The birth of a child becomes a familial gathering point, a time when many people who do not know the Lord will attend this special event. That is also true of infant dedications, where members of the family may come to the local church or to the parents home for this special occasion, even though they are not believers. It is a gathering time for the entire family and an opportunity for the pastor to share Christ.

Other public occasions include marriage ceremonies, and funerals, which have their own unique and special concerns. It can be it very helpful to have a lay person assist as a coordinator to help ease the time pressures of those special events. A wedding is an opportunity to minister the gospel of Jesus Christ. Each pastor must make their own decisions and determinations of whom they will or will not marry. Marrying one that is not born again is not permissible in many pastors' minds, because they would be blessing a union that may not be sanctioned from God's perspective. Other pastors have no concern about this at all. They feel that it is better to have them in the church hearing the gospel preached than to exclude them from church life. These are some of the personal decisions that every pastor will make, some of those decisions being determined by denominational structure.

Many families look to the pastor for assistance with wedding arrangements. It is best that a leader in the community not become too involved in intimate details. Regarding the rehearsal and the actual wedding, remember that they look to the pastor as the leader. Lead. Do not be afraid to give direction in terms of how the ceremony will flow, within the requests of the engaged couple. The different sides of the families are frequently warring over wedding details. The pastor should function, as best as possible, as a peacemaker. The ministers focus is the marrying of the couple rather than the pleasing of every member on both sides of the family. Diplomacy, coming with age and experience, eases the tensions.

Funerals can also present tense times. Often the local church looks to the pastor for most, if not all, of the organizing of a funeral service. It is imperative for a local pastor to familiarize himself with various types of funerals, and the logistical needs of a family when a death occurs. For instance, know where different funeral parlors are located, and become acquainted with the funeral directors (they are helpful allies in the planning and development of a positive funeral experience). One need not feel uncomfortable around them. The pastors responsibility goes far beyond that of just preaching the sermon. At the time of the death, the family will need care and comfort. Burial arrangements must be finalized and the funeral service planned. It is helpful to be as familiar as possible with various funeral procedures. Attend a few funerals before the occasion of the preaching of the first one arises. Observe the handling of various services, and get to know the various people within a community who are involved in a funeral service.

Other areas of public ministry include water baptisms and holy communion, especially for those churches where the first communion of a child is seen as a special observation for the family.

In any area of public ministry, the key thing to remember is that others are watching. The pastor is representing the Lord and His church to the community. Although ministers need not be legalistically bound to all of the world's standards of what they think a pastor ought to be like (such as needing a tie to mow your lawn, etc.), one still must recognize the responsibility to be men and women of character and purpose, acknowledging that the world is watching. Let each minister exercise professionalism, especially within the public arena.

THOUGHT QUESTIONS

1. Define "fiduciary," as concerns our relationship to the entire community in which we live.
2. What should be some characteristics of a pastor's life, especially as relates to being a public figure?
3. Explain a danger of emphasizing the "edifice." How can we combat this?
4. List several forms of public outreach.
5. Name the key point to remember regarding yourself and public ministry.

Chapter 12
The Leader, Pastoral Care and Counseling

The subject of pastoral care and especially counseling is massive. The past thirty years or more has seen counseling become one of the primary functions of pastors. Further, there has been a significant movement of clinical pastoral education, for the training and equipping of pastors for clinical work. It can be categorically stated that not every pastor is called to counsel. Nor is every pastor gifted in giving good counsel. But every pastor must be equipped to at least provide *some* counseling, because the clergy is the first person to whom the majority of society will turn in times of trouble.

If one is a gifted counselor who enjoys the ministry of counseling, this may not be a problem. But, as in the role of administrator, the role of counselor is one of the most problematic for pastors, for several reasons. One, most pastors are not well trained in counseling. Most Bible colleges and seminaries do not specialize in counseling, although the majority have added many courses in the area of pastoral care and counseling. For the majority of called and trained pastors, only one or two counseling ministry courses have been taken in all of his educational training. The majority of pastors are unqualified to counsel, in spite of the books they may have read. Second, a major difficulty with counseling is the time it consumes. If one pastors a church of seventy people, the pastor may be able to handle the 10% or so within the church that need to have fairly consistent counseling ministry. Being pastor and counselor of a church of more than one hundred can be extremely difficult, if not impossible, because of the additional duties that come with the role of pastor. However, since providing care and counseling is one of the historical functions of the local church and its pastor, it is necessary to plan strategically for the care of God's people, and to equip them to effectively minister to those who are hurting within society. The reasons for the dysfunction of our society is beyond the scope of this book, but needless to say the society of the Western nations is dark and broken. Recognize, however, that when people are born again, though theologically a new creation, they bring with them all of the baggage and wounds sustained in the world. They expect the church, and especially the pastor, to have all the power, tools, and ability to administer health and healing to their legitimate needs.

If pastors are not careful, especially if successful in counseling situations, they can come to believe that they are able to minister to all of those deeply wounded sheep. In fact, this ministry is the ministry of the Holy Spirit. It needs to be a ministry of *many* in the local church, rather than just one. The responsibility of the pastor is to ensure that the needs of the congregation are met to the best of his ability. The pastor will neither minister individually to each person, nor necessarily have all of the gifting essential to bring healing and wholeness to the wounded.

Dr. John McGeorge, of Ministry to Eastern Europe, summarizes the goals of pastoral care or ministry in general as follows.

First, ones goal is to help the individual believer to be all that God created him to be. Though this sounds fairly simplistic, it is in reality a primary focus. Many pastors believe that they know exactly what another individual is supposed to be like, and what they are supposed to do within the Kingdom of God. That is the height of arrogance. In truth, most of us are relatively clue-less regarding the potential of any one individual in the Body of Christ. In spite of a pastors gifting and abilities or prophetic anointing, leaders are not always able to see another's potential. Potential unfolds over time through the ministry.

Each individual, then, has a unique place, calling, and gifting within the Body of Christ. Pastors help them by providing the proper atmosphere, training, teaching and counsel, for them to become what God wants them to be, not specifically what a leader has predetermined they ought to be. Leaders must ensure that biblical standards are espoused; not ones private interpretations of the needed ingredients to cause growth to maturity of a human being. God intends that all His children be whole and complete, though less than perfect. Perfection is not a goal. Shepherds are facilitators through the local church, to help others be what God wants them to be.

The second stage is to see that a believer can do everything that God wants them to do. A person active in the Body of Christ will be happier, and more fulfilled. The sheep within the local church that are required to do nothing but sit and eat, get fat, lazy and sleepy. Leaders often see members within the local church accomplish little or nothing. Pastors can, usually unconsciously, help create this problem by not challenging them to activity.

Both men and women achieve a portion of their sense of worth from what they are able to do or accomplish. If shepherds provide them meaningful activity within their area of gifting, it will help them to significant attainments, and thus fulfill a destiny in God. Each individual is unique. Part of a shepherds responsibility is to draw out the gifting and abilities of that individual and encourage and motivate him to find a place of service in the Body of Christ and in the local community at large.

The third goal of pastoral care and ministry is to enable believers to grow in the things of God for the rest of their lives. Pastors as counselors must teach and train Christians to solve their own problems through the Word of God, to know how to study the Word and find answers in God's Word needed for their growth.
And finally, to continue to grow as a member of the Christian community, daily being transformed by the Word of God and by the power of the Holy Spirit.

Again, as stated above, it is virtually impossible for the modern-day pastor to meet all of the psychological and spiritual needs of everyone within a local church. But it is, nonetheless, the responsibility of the local pastor and elders, to train and equip people for pastoral care and counseling ministry.

It is important to have a plan or strategy for training and equipping lay leaders. Lay ministers within the Body of Christ will minister with the greatest effectiveness to other laymen and women within the local church when their equipping is strategically utilized and properly supervised. Many training programs are available to the Body of Christ, readily adaptable by the pastors for their own local church usage. Some of the key components to a lay leadership training program for pastoral care ministry are summarized below.

First, lay leaders should be men and women of maturity. They should be moving toward fulfilling the biblical requirements of an elder or a deacon, as found in the Word of God in the letters of Paul to Timothy and Titus. Look for mature believers who are able to lay aside their own needs and agenda for the sake of others. Maturity is vital; not always easy to find.

Second, there should be a screening of potential lay ministers. One of the best times to screen potential laymen is during an open seminar in the area of lay ministry or pastoral care training. The seminar will present the principles of pastoral care and counseling in a simple teaching format. During the teaching, provide a quick screening device such as a simple psychological test (For specific tools for screening, and training programs for lay ministry, contact the author) to ensure that people have the ability and stability to be able to minister to others.

Good tools are available within the Body of Christ and are fairly easy to find. Once the leadership has identified individuals who seem to have the maturity, common sense and the concern or the gift of mercy for others, plug them in to a training program that will effectively equip them for active ministry. This program does not have to be long, but should be fairly comprehensive and biblically based. II Corinthians 1:3-4 seems to strongly encourage us for lay ministry.

> *"The God of all comfort; who comforts us in all our affliction so that we may be able to comfort those who are in any affliction with the comfort with which we ourselves are comforted by God,"* **(NAS).**

The Apostle Paul is speaking to the need for believers to comfort other believers, drawing strength and empathy from the comfort that they have received in their own lives. Frequently, the best comforter or counselor is one who has already been delivered from a besetting sin or stubborn habit. Since they have walked through the process of healing in a specific area of life, they are best able to minister to others who similarly struggle.

A former alcoholic, delivered from alcoholism and showing other signs of spiritual maturity; lack of impulsivity, ability to show proper care, his house in good order, etc., is able to minister more effectively to another alcoholic, because he has "been there, done that." It is also more difficult to run games or to deceive him. In the same manner, those who have had significant losses and have overcome those losses often have greater sensitivity to those who grieve.

Thus, part of a sound leadership strategy is to find people within the Body of Christ who have the ability and maturity to care for others in areas of wounding that they have overcome. It cannot be emphasized enough the importance of using people who have overcome their own difficulties. If the pastor does not feel equipped to do the training, there are many others who can learn to care, counsel and teach. Remember that these lay counselors will come from their own slant. They will need an understanding of the overall vision of the church; the discipling of God's people which includes healing, restoration, training and equipping. The pastor remains responsible even if others conduct the training for the church

The following topics need to be taught within a lay leadership program:
- The vision of the local church.
- Who is responsible to whom within the Body of Christ.
- What is a lay minister and what is not.
- Basic skills, such as how to listen effectively, what is the role of a listening caregiver.
- Understanding of the dynamics of human behavior.
- When to pray, and how to pray effectively.

- What kind of advice to give or not give; when and if to refer.
- Basic ethics of care and counseling, such as confidentiality.
- How to minister with empathy, warmth, respect, and love.

These are necessary training tools. Every church needs a number of lay leaders who have the ability to minister, to aid in carrying the pastoral care load. Lay ministers can be effective in group or individual counsel, leading home fellowships, prayer meetings, altar ministry, and in general support of the needs of the Christian community. Because of the high level of brokenness in people's lives today and the transient nature of society, the need for positive caring pastors is greater than ever.

THE PASTOR AND HIS STAFF

Pastors, as one-man counseling operations, are rarely effective. In fact, when looking at the biblical model in the New Testament church, the raising up of lay leaders from within the church is an imperative. When the church was birthed in Jerusalem there were twelve apostles, as well as an additional one hundred eight well-trained and equipped believers. They had followed Christ at length, and understood the great commission and the teachings of Christ. The church began with a ready group of leaders who were able to minister a positive and powerful apostolic foundation upon which the first century church was built.

The Apostle Paul did not minister alone. He functioned within a team framework, or he joined a team as he did with Barnabas, in the church at Antioch. Pastoral leadership needs a team of trained and caring people to minister to the great needs of a growing church.

Why have a church staff? There are multiple tasks that must be accomplished, and, it is biblical. As already presented, the model to follow is seen in Acts chapter six. As the church grew, the workload increased and there was a desperate need for helpers.

Thus deacons were raised up for that purpose. In Acts 11:19-26, the church in Antioch had continued to grow, necessitating greater numbers of workers. God raised up workers from within for the purpose of building that local church. In Acts 13:1-2, and 5, we see Paul's first missionary journey flowing out of the church in Antioch. In that picture, the Holy Spirit sets aside the very best, the most seasoned ministers to send out. But obviously there must have been solid leadership to stay behind so that the church in Antioch could continue. Many other scriptures speak about the importance of having a multiple team for ministry. The principle of co-workers and assistants is clearly biblical.

Secondly, the reason for a staff is the demand. The tremendous demands on the pastorate require full-time, part-time, and volunteer assistants. There is only so much time for the many tasks clamoring for a pastor's attention.

What kind of problems can one find in a church staff? They are multiple. A senior pastor having over one hundred fifty people within the church will want to departmentalize it for a proper foundation for growth. Thus, the shepherd becomes the minister primarily to the department leaders and to other trained lay people who minister on his behalf. A problem can arise if the pastor has difficulty making the transition from focusing primarily upon the congregation to focusing on the leaders. Ultimately, he must become a pastor to the pastors.

Leaders must empower, equip, train, and release under-shepherds to minister effectively within the body of Christ, giving them the authority to act, within proper supervision. Another problem may stem from placing poorly trained or unqualified novices into a position of leadership that is beyond their ability. ***Absolute power corrupts absolutely***; that is especially true for those who are immature.

When an absentee pastor is not around enough to give hands-on leadership, or is primarily meeting-oriented in their ministry, then his under-shepherds may take up some of the slack and responsibility. It is natural for the sheep to begin to hear the voice of the shepherd that feeds them. Rather than seeing under-shepherds as a wonderful gift, some senior pastors see them as a threat, creating great insecurity. They *should* be insecure if their under-shepherds are novices or have proven themselves disloyal. But if they have well trained and equipped their under-shepherds, who understand their role, and they have properly supervised them, then the inter-staff relations should be a great blessing to everyone involved.

How can one build good staff relations? How can a pastor empower and assist lay leaders? First of all, it is good to inform the local fellowship about the responsibilities of each lay minister or staff member. Second, see that every member of the staff clearly understands each other's responsibilities for proper coordination. The staff members should know who supervises them, and for whom they are responsible. And third, a seasoned leader will allow changes in the responsibilities of the staff as situations change. Job descriptions are wonderful, but they ought not be set in concrete.

Building a better church staff is basically a matter of building better interpersonal relations. It begins with the pastor. What the church staff will be like depends upon the pastor manifesting the fruit of the Holy Spirit in his or her life. Thus, if the pastor has a right relationship with the Lord, and is continuously working on positive relations with those in positions of authority, then the work of God will progress with relative smoothness. If the pastor is faithful, meek, and self-controlled, the staff will follow suit.

How do leaders properly supervise a local staff? A shepherd must do so with understanding. A pastor needs to seek to understand the people with whom they labor. Become acquainted with each one individually, whether selected and trained by the pastor, or inherited from another's ministry and tested over time to ensure faithfulness. Shepherds are wise to recognize that everyone is different. Thank the Lord for that. Wouldn't it be a frightening thought if everyone were just like the pastor! Understand, accept and appreciate these differences. This does not mean to allow or tolerate areas of sin, but uniqueness. Secondly, leaders are to learn to appreciate and respect those with whom they co-labor. One cannot expect a new staff member to fully understand the vision, or to fully mature overnight. It has taken the Lord many years to mature the seasoned leader and it will take time for others as well. Thus, show appreciation for those who are staff, and newly developing leaders, without jealousy. A spirit of jealousy or suspicion can be one of the greatest problems in many churches. The enviousness, power struggles and political maneuvering which frequently affect the church really do flow from the senior pastor. If the senior pastor is secure in his or her position, and the lay leaders have been well-equipped, trained and qualified biblically to be leaders, the staff will tend to function positively.

Thirdly, another focus of positive supervision is that of clear communication. It is important to meet regularly with the staff and communicate clearly what the goals and expectations are. Also have times of fellowship and open communication without the stress of tasks hanging over their heads. Ultimately, positive supervision means encouragement that flows from the senior pastor to the under shepherds.

THE BUILDING OF ELDERS

No church can function without deacons or church servants. Churches need ushers, greeters, maintenance personnel and helpers to maintain the buildings and grounds. Churches need Sunday School teachers. The church has many needs, and so does the pastor. Shepherds primarily need under-pastors to come alongside and function as part of an "eldership" team. All Christian leaders understand that the head of the church is Christ. Christ has given to His body the Five-Fold Ministry team that have the primary responsibility of equipping God's people to bring them to maturity.

Within local churches, God raises up a plurality of elders that have the ability to shepherd the flock of God. These are men and women who have proven godliness, good reputations and the ability to teach in the body of Christ.

> *"Remember them which have the rule over you, who have spoken to you the Word of God; whose faith follow, considering the end of their conversation,"* **(Hebrews 13:7 KJV).**
>
> *"Obey them that have the rule over you and submit yourselves: for they watch for your souls as they that must give an account, that they may do it with joy and not grief, for that is unprofitable for you,"* **(Hebrews 13:17 KJV).**

In these verses of Scripture, elders are to lead and to teach. They are to be a model of the faith of God in front of the church community. Promoting one to an elder before the proper testing of character may give him a weapon for control and power. An elder needs to first prove his eldership, the ability to humbly lead, recognizing one's responsibility to the flock of God. Sheep are happy to obey leaders who love, feed, and care for them. Sheep scatter when a shepherd or under-shepherd has a hidden agenda, or a primary goal of control and power.

All shepherds need to meet the qualifications of leadership, be strong in doctrine, etc. Once placed into an area of leadership as elders, they need to be given the responsibility and opportunity to minister effectively within the Body of Christ.

How are elders selected? The Bible indicates that they were raised up from within the local church. Generally, as with deacons, they would be men or women who had already proven themselves by consistent and faithful service over time. That faithfulness must be demonstrated. The senior pastor must be in relationship with men and women who have a desire for leadership, able to observe them in real life settings (not just at church).

Often the task of raising up elders fails because the pastor fails to build leaders in the church. Dr. Howard Ryan of Church Enrichment Ministries, gives eleven steps for the discipling of elders. They are provided with commentary:

1. Begin with a Bible study for men and women who want

to move into areas of leadership. Included should be those who desire to be elders and potential leaders in various areas of ministry. This is a select group, chosen by the local pastor. Look for men and women who are available, teachable, and have a heart for the Lord.

2. Teach biblical theology. It provides a solid foundation, both doctrinally and in understanding how Scripture applies to the church. Theological teaching should be simple, clear and systematic.

3. Train them to relate God's word to all areas of life. As Spurgeon suggested, their blood should become "bibling." That is, pastors should show them how to solve problems and answer questions with scriptural principles.

4. Share the heart of the pastor as well as ones mind. Give them the passion for Christ and His church. Share the joys and frustrations of pastoral oversight. Through this true leaders will have hearts knit together with the pastors and with the vision that God has given the leadership for the local church.

5. Make them feel a part of every significant decision that is made. Not only is there wisdom in such counsel, but it will also train them to make decisions within a biblical framework. Leaders in team rise and fall together; none stands alone. They will learn to share responsibility through that process.

6. Spend time with them individually, apart from scheduled meetings. Go to dinner with the family or share recreational times together. This weaves together the leaders personal lives, and provides a forum for observation away from church.

7. Confront and admonish. Face their failures with love and encouragement. Be honest in the process. This builds greater openness. The pastor should be cautiously vulnerable him/herself when falling short of perfection.

8. Give them a sending responsibility. This gives them the opportunity to develop and prove their leadership. Challenge them to take the initiative. Share mutual input in the plans and struggles for ministry. This is a good time to teach them biblical principles of leadership. Give each man or woman a small area of ministry

and watch them grow in their abilities, gradually adding new areas as they evidence skill and commitment.

9. Pray for the elders. They will stay on the shepherds heart and give God a chance to glorify Himself in their lives.

10. Be willing to sacrifice for them. It may mean early morning prayer, discipling sessions, phone conversations, listening to their reports, sharing their struggles, bringing your skill to bear in their needs. The pastor will communicate how much they love them and how highly esteemed they are by intentional focused interest.

11. Most of all, set the example, which is the basis of ministerial integrity and credibility. If the shepherd fails in various tasks, they can be overcome with a godly example. One cannot overcome if there is a failed life pattern.

It is important to focus on providing the atmosphere whereby the elders might grow. This begins from the time they are born again until they mature into church leadership.

PROPER RELATIONSHIPS

As love flows from respect within marriage, so it is with pastoral care and ministry. The pastor of a local church should be respected as the spiritual overseer of the flock. They function with many hats; chairman of the board of the corporation, spiritual leader and advisor, primary preacher of the oracles of God, the prophetic voice in the congregation, to name a few. Elders indeed, that is, of proven character, faithfulness and gifting in the Body of Christ, and deacons, called to service, full of the Holy Ghost and on fire for God, need to show proper respect to the pastor, both publicly and privately.

The pastor is not infallible. Part of every believers relationships as members of the body of Christ, is to be able to confront and bring correction to each other. That openness to correction is missing in many independent denominational churches, where a heavy control is placed in the role of the pastor. All must be in balance. There must be respect for the pastor, and simultaneously a respect from the pastor for the lay leaders who are working with him. The elders of the early church, also called bishops, overseers, pastors, shepherds or guides, to whom was delegated the responsibility of ruling or the oversight of the church, speak of this (I Tim 3:1-7, 5:17-19, and Titus 1:5-10).

The deacons were their helpers (Acts 7 and I Tim 3:8-13). They were servants who worked in rudimentary areas of service within the local church. Their authority was delegated to them by the eldership. The elders gave overall governmental oversight of every aspect of the local fellowship. Elders and deacons will each have specialized areas of gifting and ability, being each created differently.

Part of the role of leadership, especially the pastor, is to determine who has potential for being a deacon, an elder, or other leader. Once this is discovered, the focus becomes the equipping of the saints, both in areas of character, as well as in the knowledge of God's Word. Pastors train deacons and elders to function in their area of ministry. Once proven character is seen and various gifts begin to come to the forefront, the pastor's responsibility is to place them within their ministry, where they will begin to function under proper supervision. Those that prove themselves faithful over time are able to move into greater areas of responsibility. If they have been well trained and equipped, they will learn the same model of training and searching for leadership and continue the discipleship process, thus building the kingdom of God.

Pastoral care is a very difficult and important area of ministry, for a simple reason. The people of God, brought out of darkness into light, are characterized by God's Word as sheep. They are easily scattered. Yet they want, beyond anything else, to relate to a shepherd who loves them, who leads, feeds, and corrects them when needed. They need a shepherd who is there for them, providing the stability that they may not get in any other avenue of life. Most visionary pastors miss this area of ministry, causing great disturbances and a lack of true spiritual growth in the sheep. Without adequate shepherding, the sheep do not grow in the characteristics of the Kingdom of God (righteousness, peace and joy in the Holy Ghost). Thus, it is inherent upon a senior pastor, regardless of leadership style, to be actively involved in training and equipping men and women of God for effective service so that they can care for the needs of others within the Body of Christ.

THOUGHT QUESTIONS

1. If a pastor is not gifted in counseling, what should he do?
2. What are the goals of pastoral ministry?
3. How should you select lay leaders for assisting in pastoral ministry? What do you teach these lay leaders?
4. What might be a reason for difficulty in raising up elders in a church?
5. List Dr. Howard's 11 steps for discipling elders.

Chapter 13
The Pastoral Pitfalls

In this chapter some of a pastor's potential pitfalls are presented to provide understanding and assistance in avoiding the difficulties that many fellow brethren have had over the past few years.

I overheard a group of pastors talking about areas of potential pastoral pitfalls. Laughingly, they stated girls, greed and golf. The third is not golf, it is glory! In reality, those *are* Satan's three primary modern tools he uses to tempt men and women of God with. The Scriptures designate them *the lust of the flesh, the lust of the eyes, and the pride of life* (I John 2:16). No spiritual leader is exempt from these areas of temptation. Even Christ Himself was tempted in all of these areas, yet without sin. It is important to take a close look at these three areas, *the lust of the flesh, the lust of the eyes, and the pride of life*, in order to, as Solomon admonished his boys:

"Keep your heart with all diligence; for out of it flow the issues of life," (Proverbs 4:23 KJV).

First of all, one area of concern can potentially be the pleasures of life. God created mankind with the ability and appetite for pleasure. However, many things can be detractors from our call in the Lord. Simple things, such as hobbies that should be productive and helpful, can become a consuming passion for many pastors. Ministers of the Gospel are people of purpose. Hobbies can be helpful, as can any area of pleasure, but it should never distract us from our primary purpose in the things of God. Pleasures that are often legitimate but not always expedient, can lead us away from our primary focus. Various sports, hunting, fishing, even golf, can be considered a detractor if they take too much time and precedence in a spiritual leaders life.

Shepherds must take care in terms of the company that they

choose, as well as places of entertainment that they frequent. Many leaders have the liberty to attend a movie or enjoy a restaurant with an attached bar. Fifty years ago, that would not have been as acceptable. Remember that people are watching their leaders; take care not to be a stumbling block to a weaker sheep. Leaders also need to guard against fatigue, which breaks down the normal defenses against temptation.

Another area of great potential pitfall is that of morals. The Bible says in II Tim. 2:22, that all Christians are to flee youthful lusts. It doesn't say to try and fight it. Only in fleeing or running from lust can a leader avoid the power of its temptation. As men and women of God, be extremely careful not to be drawn into areas of sexual temptation. Avoid the very appearance of evil (I Thes. 5:22). Be honest, tell the truth and be above reproach in every business dealing.

There is a real need to guard our morals in front of others. Be especially careful in how one treats members of the opposite sex, in speech and familiarity, because intentions can be misinterpreted. Ones dress and habits should be modest. Concern for how others see leadership should not become a paranoid preoccupation. However, caution is always judicious.

MINISTERIAL INTEGRITY

The Bible speaks of several areas of integrity, especially for leaders. Here are some of the most important for leaders to be concerned with. First, a pastor should be chaste. The minister is the representative of the kingdom of God. As such, they must always be concerned about their name and reputation in front of the community. As mentioned above, circumspect behavior in all private and public dealings, both in business, and in personal relationships should be a part of the pastors life and walk. Secondly, shepherds must be scrupulously honest. Specifically, pastors need to pay their bills. If through misfortune one becomes overwhelmed with debt, they need to make every effort to pay all of their bills. A pastors word should be his bond. When entering into a covenant agreement or a contract with someone, fulfill it, whether that be a pledge made for missions, a business dealing, the purchase of a car or a home, or consumer credit.

Caution would dictate that one avoid entering into business with members of the pastors own local church. Lay leaders are often happy to help in a time of difficulty for the local pastor. At the same time, it is amazing how quickly friends part company when it comes down to simple things like *money*. Thus, avoid any entanglements, whether it be through business, or loans, etc., from members of ones own congregation.

In terms of overall integrity, all leaders must carefully utilize the time the Lord has given. The pastor is not really his own boss, though in many ways it may appear so. Shepherds must be submitted to the lordship of Christ and to others within the Body of Christ. There is much to be done in ministry. Most pastors have no difficulty with that reality; in fact, most pastors work fifty to fifty-five hours every week, week in and week out. A few have learned to skip in areas of responsibility and do not show integrity in terms of time commitments.

When leading and feeding the flock, do so with the purpose of fully caring for them, not just for financial gain.

> *"Shepherd the flock of God among you, exercising oversight not under compulsion, but voluntarily, according to the will of God; and not for sordid gain, but with eagerness; nor yet as lording it over those allotted to your charge, but proving to be examples to the flock. And when the Chief Shepherd appears, you will receive the unfading crown of glory,"* **(I Pet. 5:2-4 NAS).**

Thus, spiritual leaders are to be faithful in keeping stated office hours. Further, they should be faithful to ensure that proper supervision and follow-up on personal commitments are made. When a pastor does not keep to commitments made, they lose much of their salt and light ability with the congregation. These are all issues of integrity. Integrity is one of the few things that pastors have in terms of ministry.

Some other practical advice would include the need to avoid secular entanglements. Many love to merchandise the gospel. Guard against the temptation to divide time between spiritual ministry and secular pursuits for personal advantage. There is no sin in secular employment for the minister where it is needed. When the church provides a proper livelihood, the minister's time should be devoted to advancing the kingdom of God.

II Tim. 2:4 says, *"No man that goes to war entangles himself with the affairs of this life. But they work so they might please Him who has chosen him to be a soldier."*

Our loyalty is to Christ. With the pastor's great privilege of serving the flock of God comes an equally great responsibility. A pastors hope is to live their life in such a way that others will follow them as they follow Christ (I Cor. 11:1).

Taking care what one says, especially when sharing about someone within the local church, needs to be a pastors policy. My childhood pastor had a very small counseling load. Why? We always knew who he had counseled the week previously! That individual would come up in the sermon the following Sunday. When people realize that their confidences would be broken, or if they feel their personal lives are treated disdainfully or flippantly by the local leader, people will not come for care or counsel. Thus, the need to guard our tongues is self-evident.

Many spiritual leaders would rather not talk about the things of God when they get together. It is like talking "shop." Instead, they want to talk about their golf score or the latest jokes. It is fairly common in every area of life to relieve stress by talking irreverently. But leaders in spiritual oversight need to be very careful that their focus be primarily on the things of God.

Avoid a party spirit. Leaders should avoid taking sides in

petty quarrels or controversies because pastors are shepherds of the whole flock. All human beings are subject to influence to some degree.

All people, no matter how spiritual, have natural sympathies, likes and dislikes. Some members of the congregation will always be more likable than others. Beware the taking of sides, for it can actually ruin ones ministry. Shepherds must be servants of all.

The people God allows the pastor to minister to deserve attention and care. One cannot minister effectively to someone that is unknown or unfamiliar. While avoiding familiarity, the minister must live close to his people. Their hearts need consistent care. Let me re-emphasize: This cannot be done from the pulpit alone, in spite of the importance of prayer and ministry of the Word. Pastors, need to be involved with the congregation, to learn about them, know them, and understand them to the best of ones ability. The large church pastor can at least ensure that the needs of the people are being adequately provided for, as discussed in the previous chapter.

Time can be a major problem for pastors. Leaders must plan ahead for all services. In I Cor. 14:40 it says, *"Let all things be done decently and in order."* Shepherds need to prepare for the local service. Many pastors feel that their anointing will be affected if they meet people prior to the beginning of a service. Some, generally out of insecurity, will avoid being to the service on time, or will come in fifteen to twenty minutes late. They then wonder why so many others straggle in late as well. Sheep will follow their shepherd. The habits that the leader has will often be reflected in the children that God provides to them.

They will follow a leaders example. Nothing makes a better impression than being business-like, prompt and alert. This is especially true of a minister of the gospel of Jesus Christ. Pastors must discipline themselves. All humans, including dynamic Holy Ghost filled ministers have various areas of weaknesses. However, as the Apostle Paul proclaimed, where I am weak, there I am strong (because of the grace of God flowing through his life).

Finally, a leader must keep their bodies under subjection.

> ***"I bring...my body into subjection: lest...when I have preached to others, I myself should be disqualified," (I Cor. 9:27).***

In summary, the primary pitfalls of pastoral care and ministry can be seen in one of three areas, the lust of the flesh, the lust of the eyes, and the pride of life.

The lust of the flesh refers to ones desire to fulfill the needs of ones own life, physically and emotionally. Pastoral ministry is extremely intense, active, and difficult. It would be easy to neglect ones own physical needs. These include the sexual needs that are common to all men and women. Of course, God intended for these needs to be met within the relationship of marriage, and it is important to make sure that these needs are cared for in a balanced fashion. Many a male leader has been led or wandered into sin resulting in serious and permanent consequences due to the lack of attention to these basic needs.

Loneliness greatly increases one's vulnerability. A pastor involved in counseling ministry, an evangelist traveling during an extended outreach ministry can become easy prey to the devil in areas of loneliness. After feelings of loneliness or spousal neglect, it is easy to allow one's mind to wander into areas of fantasy, and into temptation to fulfill the lust of the flesh.

Many men of God would never submit themselves to adultery or fornication because of fear of the consequences. But they will often sublimate those feelings and needs. Instead of dealing with the poor relationship with their spouse and the need for counseling care and healing, they will instead sublimate it into other areas of "isms," (such as alcoholism, workaholism, foodaholism, or even adrenalinism). The later is especially insidious, and can be seen in the need for constant high pressure, high powered services to feed those feelings of inadequacy or loneliness that have developed due to a lack of fulfillment within the sexual arena of life. These things must be talked about and cared for in pastoral ministry. Make no mistake: All leaders are subject to temptations of the flesh. Again, this is why leaders must guard their hearts. Guarding ones heart and mind comes through proper accountability and a willingness to submit to counsel and accountability from others in the Body of Christ.

The second area is the lust of the eyes. The Word still says, "Thou shalt not covet." Covetousness continues to be a major problem, especially within the church. There is nothing inherently wrong in a pastor having a nice home, car, and a relatively comfortable lifestyle, if available. These may be gifts from God to enjoy and share. But spiritual leaders often justify their greed by cloaking it in religion. Pastors want to build a larger church for the Kingdom of God. They want a bigger car so that they can transport more people, and yet they never transport them. The justification of covetousness, jealousy, and the desire to have other people's goods can be overheard at most any leaders conference. Pastors even covet others' spiritual gifts of God. Leaders so need to guard their hearts, and be very careful not to sin the sin of covetousness. To harbor the lust of the eyes can be a major pitfall for those in full-time service, blocking the fulfillment of ones destiny in God.

The last is the pride of life. Once a pastor obtains their goals, comfort can be a real downfall. If one places their self-worth in titles and positions, the size of their congregation, or anything other than Jesus Christ and Him crucified, a downfall is on its way. Shepherds *are* aware that pride comes before a fall. Pride says, "You have nothing to say to me because my ministry is bigger than your ministry." It says, "I'm not open to your correction; you are not a part of *my* denominational structure." Pride prevents growth and dwarfs ones spiritual life. Pastors approach the eve of their own destruction any time they allow the sin of pride, especially in ones own life achievements, to enter their heart.

These are the primary pitfalls that face every leader. The devil loves to destroy or strike the shepherd. If given the chance, he will divide, conquer, and scatter the sheep.

Today God is bringing change to the church. He is shifting

the focus away from being independent local churches or representing a certain denomination within a community. Rather, there is a growing realization of just how much pastors in a locality need one another. Leaders must learn to be mutually and relationally accountable to one another and assist each other, in order not to fall into the pitfalls that have wreaked havoc and destruction to the Body of Christ.

THOUGHT QUESTIONS

1. All pastoral pitfalls fall within 3 broad categories. Name them and give the Bible reference.
2. List some areas in life to beware.
3. Name 4 areas in which a pastor must maintain integrity.
4. What seemingly minor pitfall can actually ruin your ministry?

Chapter 14
The Pastor and His Passion

Paul, the New Testament apostle, was a skilled shepherd. Christ also is our Chief Shepherd. These two examples paint well the picture of a worthy shepherd and his priorities. Christ exhibited His passion in His championing the cause of women, His tremendous love for children, His ministry to the poor and oppressed of the devil, and His deep love for the Father and the Apostles that gave their lives to follow Him.

The Apostle Paul, who barely considered himself worthy to be considered with the saints, gave everything he had for the sake of the Gospel. No sacrifice was too great, in light of so great a salvation through Christ. He did not consider his beatings, rejection, and abandonment much for him to endure, for Christ was everything to him. Paul was a man who loved the church, prayed for it, wrote letters of encouragement and direction, and by the end of his life, could only proclaim,

"...that I may know Him, and the power of His resurrection, and the fellowship of His sufferings, being conformed to His death." (Phil. 3:10)

Pastors begin their ministry with a great deal of passion, zeal and vision to see the Kingdom of God expanded here on earth. They start with great intentions. Some of these ministries end prematurely, the pastors burned out, hurt, or even shamed. This is not the plan of God. God's plan is for His called co-laborers to continuously grow in the things of God and fulfill a great destiny as leaders take their place in the Body of Christ. There are several areas of passion on which a pastor needs to focus.

First, a pastor needs to have a passion for God and His Word. Needless to say, the Word of God is necessary for one's own strength and edification. All leaders need their spiritual fires stoked in the Word in order to fulfill the responsibility to preach as the oracles of God. Pastors are to bring forth a fresh word in time and season that will nurture, strengthen, guide and direct the sheep that God has called into ones pasture. The passion for God's Word and the revelation that is received through intense and consistent study, must always be stirred up within Gods' men and women. One of the best ways to stir up that passion is by supplementing Scripture reading with other books that speak about Scripture, especially from great writers of times past. Every pastor has his own favorites. Reading authors that edify, enlighten, and increase ones awareness of the magnificence of God are by far the best. Further, reading great literature of any kind can lift the mind of the Pastor from the mundane to the sublime. Tackling some Shakespeare or other great writers in diverse areas of interest broaden ones intellectual and spiritual perspective.

Godly passion can also be stirred as one dialogues with other pastors about revelation that they are receiving from the Word of God. It is important to have an open mind, heart, and spirit, yet to also be willing to test Scripture with Scripture, and to grow in the things of God.

Secondly, shepherds need a passion for prayer. There has been a refreshing reminder of the vital place for prayer over the last few years. Ones first and foremost responsibility as pastors is to worship the Lord and to commune with Him. Of vital importance is the setting aside of special time to be alone with Him. Not only must one stir up a passionate prayer life and develop that deeper walk and intimacy with the Lord individually, but leaders must seek to stir up the ministry of prayer amongst one another as brethren in the Body of Christ. All over the United States and in many parts of the world, prayer groups of pastors and other spiritual leaders are springing up, almost spontaneously. There is a greater sense that the church in the locality is more important than the individual local church. Pastors are learning to love each other as they begin to vulnerably pray with one another. This greater sense of passion helps inspire and carry Gods' leaders through difficult times in ministry.

Third, pastors must be passionate about the people of God.

God's people are precious. Remember, as stated earlier in this book, that every shepherd has a flock to oversee. In Proverbs 27:23-27 it says;

> *"Know well the condition of your flocks, and pay attention to your herds; for riches are not forever, nor does a crown endure to all generations. When the grass disappears, the new growth is seen, and the herbs of the mountains are gathered in, the lambs will be for your clothing, and the goats will bring the price of a field, and there will be goats' milk enough for your food, for the food of your household, and sustenance for your excellence, and in your moral excellence knowledge."*

> *"Therefore, brethren, be all the more diligent to make certain about His calling and choosing you; for as long as you practice these things, you will never stumble,"* **(II Peter 1:10).**

Not only does pastoral leadership require diligence in ones passion for God's people, but it is needed to care for them watchfully, to ensure that they eat a steady and a healthy spiritual diet, and to protect them from outside intruders that would take them in a wrong direction.

A leaders passion needs to be focused on the things that are most important. Whatever one attends to, ones family, ones work, the stock exchange, or ones golf game, ultimately reveals where the heart is and what is considered to be treasure. Beware: Focusing on the needs of the people to increase one's wealth can lead to destruction. God provides for His own, both through the sheep, which tend to follow the voice of the shepherd and provide the fleece, but also through the independent goats, who are worth a very great price. God intends to bless, minister to, and fill the shepherds' needs through both the sheep and the goats that God gathers as ones faithful ministry unfolds.

Lastly, ones passion should be towards the establishment of the Kingdom of God. Jesus came, and John the Baptist before him, preaching the Kingdom of God. The Apostle Paul preached on the Kingdom of God. As ministers of the gospel, the goal is to see the Kingdom of God fully established here on earth, that when Christ returns, He will have a church without spot or wrinkle over which to reign. The Kingdom of God is the churches concern and should be its passion. Regardless of ones theological position about what the Kingdom of God is, it was the consummate focus of Christ' ministry and preaching. How can any leader neglect such a powerful mandate form the pattern of New Testament ministry? God would have us as men and women of God, focus on the establishment of the kingdom and the reign of Christ here on earth. This is accomplished through church planting, unity, prayer, tearing down strongholds, through all the activities of pastoral ministry. Remember that ones passion should not be on buildings or on building a large ministry for oneself. If God provides that, so much more the blessing. But the ultimate focus is on the building and establishment of God's Kingdom in the lives of people who are coming out of darkness into the light.

    The ministry of a Pastor, or for that matter, any Five-fold ministry leader, is a tremendous responsibility. Truly, there is no more difficult assignment with greater potential for problems and joy than the ministry. The prayer of every leader should be for their fellow laborer, whatever the label or dress, whatever the strength or weakness. Leaders need each other and the support of men and women who God gathers to see the glorious work of the Lord Jesus Christ completed.

THOUGHT QUESTIONS

1. A pastor needs to be passionate about 4 areas; name them.
2. Why is a passion for God and His Word extremely important?
3. In what ways does prayer contribute to our ministry?
4. Our passion for god's people is characterized how?
5. How can we further the establishment of the Kingdom of God on earth?

BIBLIOGRAPHY

Adams, Jay E., *Shepherding God's Flock*. Grand Rapids: Zondervan, 1974.

Covey, Stephen R., *The Seven Habits of Highly Effective People*. New York: Simon and Schuster, 1989.

Chant, Th.D., Ken, *Building the Church God Wants*. Ramona: Vision Publishing, 1994.

Chant, Th.D., Ken, *The Pentecostal Pulpit*. Ramona: Vision Publishing, 1995.

DeKoven, Ph.D., Stan E., *Journey to Wholeness*. Ramona: Vision Publishing, 1992.

DeKoven, Ph.D., Stan E., *Marriage and Family Life*. Ramona: Vision Publishing, 1989.

DeKoven, Ph.D., Stan E., *On Belay*. Ramona: Vision Publishing, 1991.

Gangel, Kenneth O., *Feeding and Leading*. Wheaton: Victor, 1989.

MacArthur, Jr., John, *Rediscovering Pastoral Ministry*. Dallas: Word, 1995.

Sanders, J. Oswald, *Spiritual Leadership*. Rev. Ed., Chicago: Moody, 1980.

Spurgeon, Charles Hadden, *Lectures to My Students*. Reprint, Grand Rapids: Baker, 1977.

Wiersbe, Warren W. and Wiersbe, David, *Making Sense of the Ministry* 2d ed. Grand Rapids: Baker, 1989.

Zimmerman, Ph.D., Thomas F., Carlson D.D., G. Raymond, Bicket, Ph.D., Zenas J. eds., *And He Gave Pastors: Pastoral Theology in Action*, Springfield: Gospel Publishing House, 1979.

APPENDIX

* Our thanks to Bay Ridge Christian Center, Brooklyn, NY for allowing us to use their mission statement/annual report for a model.

SAMPLE MISSION STATEMENT VISION CHRISTIAN CENTER INTERNATIONAL

*The purpose of **Vision Christian Center International** is to bring people into agreement with God and one another, by virtue of an orderly wholeness, through the following channels:*

WORSHIP UNTO GOD DISCIPLESHIP FELLOWSHIP SERVICE
PURPOSE AND VISION OF VISION CHRISTIAN CENTER INTERNATIONAL*

MISSION PURPOSE STATEMENT

WORSHIP
To grow into a "fully devoted lifestyle" unto Jesus Christ in all areas of our lives.

DISCIPLESHIP
To reconcile or win over the believer and/or the unbeliever to God towards accepting the responsibility of God's chief interest here on earth as a marked disciple of Jesus Christ.

FELLOWSHIP
To create a lifestyle of sharing, companionship, and support as a tool to serve one another and express Christian love in tangible ways.

SERVICE
Develop channels of service to the community of San Diego and

the Body of Christ at Vision Christian Center International. These channels will be in the area of:

MINISTRY AND SERVICE OF VCCI

The following ministries of Vision Christian Center International are a visible expression of our four-fold purpose as a church.

WORSHIP
1. Adult Choir
2. Children's Choir
3. Early Morning and Evening Prayer
4. Musicians/Worship Singers
5. Sunday Celebration Service

DISCIPLESHIP
1. Children's Church
2. Seminars
3. Sunday Bible School
4. Vision International University
5. Wed. Discipleship Class
6. Wed. Membership Class

FELLOWSHIP
1. Home Care Groups
2. Women's Fellowship
3. Singles Fellowship
4. Sports Ministry
5. Married Couples Fellowship
6. Men's Fellowship
7. Annual Retreats
8. Young Adolescence
9. Youth
10. Young Adults

SERVICE
1. Altar Workers

2. Audio Ministry
3. Evangelistic Teams
4. Fund Raising
5. Helps Ministry
6. Hospitality
7. Mercy Missions
8. Nursery
9. Vision Bookstore
10. Printing Ministry
11. Prison Ministry
12. Radio
13. Senior Saints Ministry
14. Transportation
15. Ushers/Greeters
16. Videos

VISION CHRISTIAN CENTER INTERNATIONAL ACCOMPLISHMENTS IN THE YEAR 2005

ACCOMPLISHMENTS IN THE YEAR 2005

WORSHIP
1. Celebrated special Easter services jointly with six other churches.
2. The church choir was reorganized.

DISCIPLESHIP
1. Our Prayer Warriors participated in a Seminar with Dr. Peter Wagner.
2. Developed personal "New Beginnings Program" for one on one discipleship.
3. The leadership of our Home Care Groups attended the Institute of Church Growth Seminar.
4. Vision Bible Institute graduated 18 students from its various

programs.
5. Began 12 step recovery ministry in conjunction with Retoration Ranch ministry.

FELLOWSHIP
1. Started our Home Care Groups with cells.
2. Annual Church Picnic Day at Ramona Community Park.

SERVICE
1. Blessed New Life Christian Fellowship with a $1,000 offering for their building fund.
2. Participated in the Annual Convention of the Chrisco Churches in Kenya, Africa. Dr. DeKoven conducted a leadership seminar for a large group of church leaders.
3. Celebrated our Friend Day with great success.
4. Our Nursery Ministry celebrates God's creation.
5. Profession of Faith and Rededication -21
6. Water Baptism - 10
7. Baby Dedication - 8
8. Marriage - 4
9. Bookstore expanded its service.
10. Mercy Missions continues its labor of love and work of faith by ministering to the homeless and destitute.
11. On Thanksgiving Day shared in ministering to the poor in partnership with New Life Christian Fellowship and Pastor George Runyan.
12. Expanded our office by adding a full-time Executive Administrator in the person of Maureen Kelley, M.A.
13. Special Pastor's Appreciation weekend services.
14. Gave out over one hundred gifts to children of inmates in the penal institutions of our city as part of the Angel Tree Project, a co-venture with Prision Fellowship.

CAPITAL INVESTMENT
1. Replaced Air Conditioning System
2. Remodeled the new Administrive Office.

3. Moved the trailer and repared it for ministry use.
4. Purchased a new copier to serve all the ministries of the church.
5. Continued to upgrade our computer system.

VISION CHRISTIAN CENTER INTERNATIONAL ORGANIZATIONAL CHART

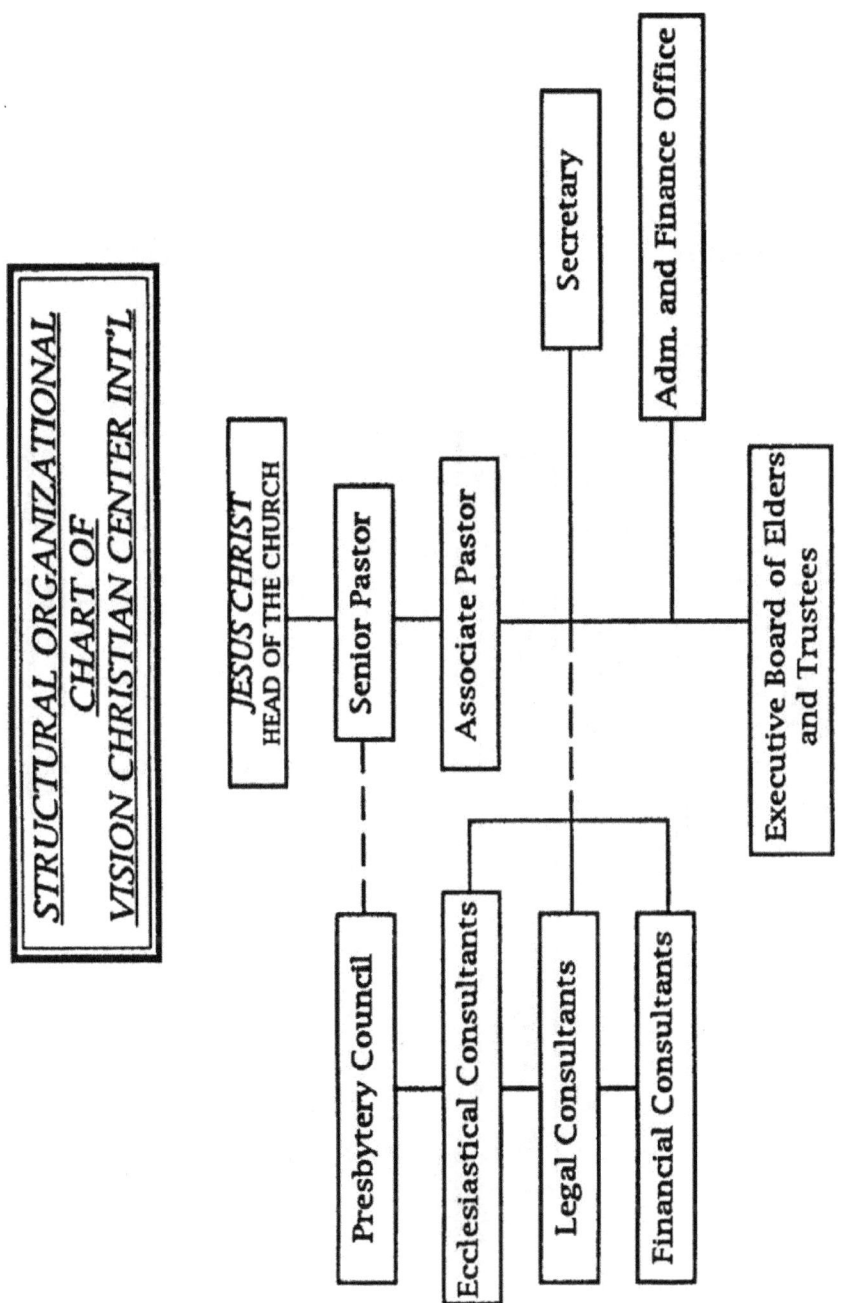

Leadership in the Church

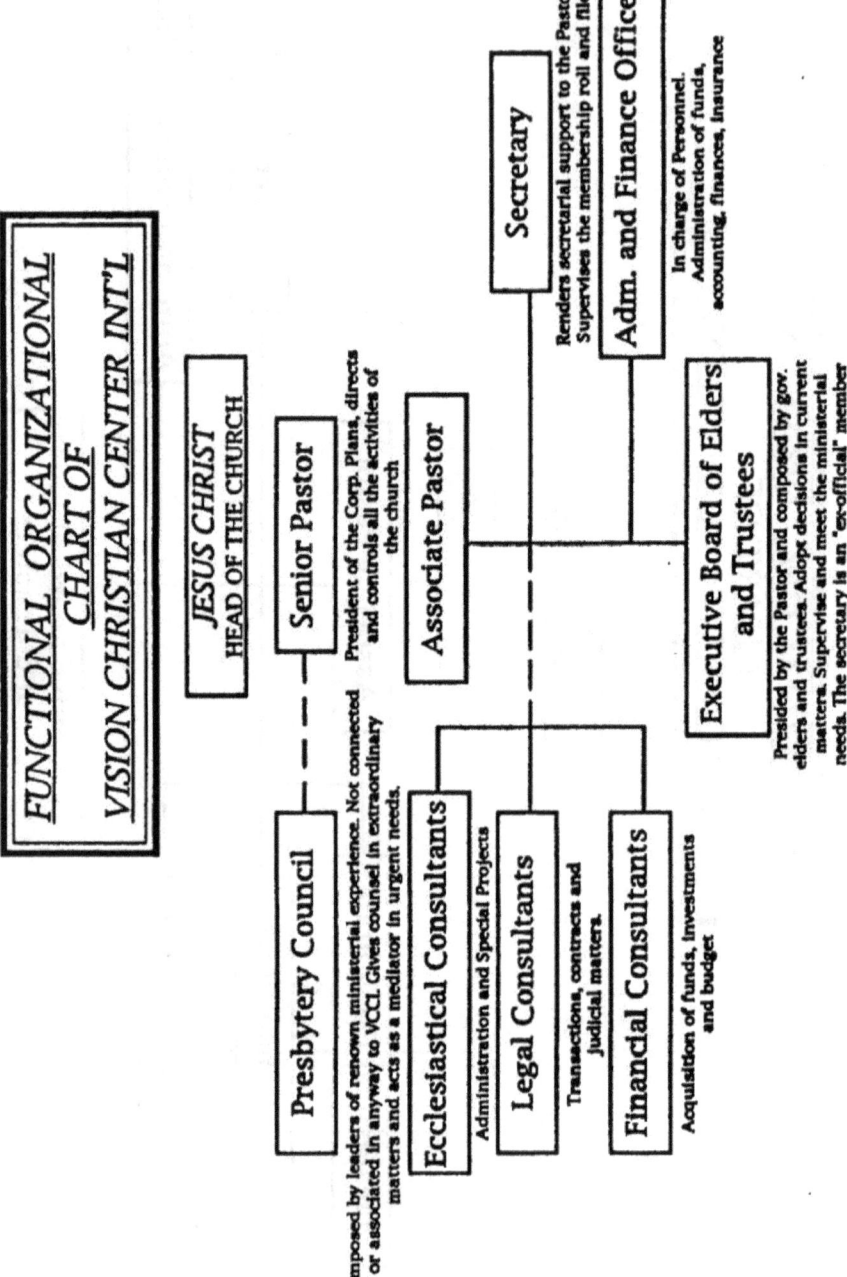

SENIOR PASTOR

EXECUTIVE BOARD OF ELDERS & TRUSTEES

DEPARTMENTS

| WORSHIP/PRAISE | ADMINISTRATION | COMMUNICATIONS/PRINTING | EDUCATION | CELL GROUPS |

MISSIONS | MINISTERIAL SERVICE

FRATERNITIES

| CHILDREN | WOMEN | MARRIED COUPLES | MENS | SINGLES | YOUTH |

THE CHURCH

...and are of God's Household, having been built upon the foundation of the apostles and prophets, Christ Jesus Himself, being the cornerstone.
Ephesians 2:19-20

VISION CHRISTIAN CENTER INTERNATIONAL DIRECTORY OF MINISTRY LEADERS

SENIOR PASTOR

Joe Pastor 1234 Anystreet Anytown, USA 12345

SENIOR ELDERS

John Senior Elder 1234 Anystreet Anytown, USA 12345	Paul Senior Elder 1234 Anystreet Anytown, USA 12345

GOVERNING ELDERS

Joe Governing Elder 1234 Anystreet Anytown, USA 12345	John Governing Elder 1234 Anystreet Anytown, USA 12345	Paul Governing Elder 1234 Anystreet Anytown, USA 12345

ELDER

Joe Elder 1234 Anystreet Anytown, USA 12345

TRUSTEES

Joe Trustee 1234 Anystreet Anytown, USA 12345	John Trustee 1234 Anystreet Anytown, USA 12345	Paul Trustee 1234 Anystreet Anytown, USA 12345

Leadership in the Church

MINISTERS

Minister of Children Joe Director 1234 Anystreet Anytown, USA 12345 (123) 456-7890	Minister of Evangelism Joe Director 1234 Anystreet Anytown, USA 12345 (123) 456-7890
Minister of Missions Joe Director 1234 Anystreet Anytown, USA 12345 (123) 456-7890	Minister of Children Joe Director 1234 Anystreet Anytown, USA 12345 (123) 456-7890

WORSHIP

Adult Choir Joe Director 1234 Anystreet Anytown, USA 12345 (123) 456-7890	Children's Choir Joe Director 1234 Anystreet Anytown, USA 12345 (123) 456-7890
Musicians Joe Director 1234 Anystreet Anytown, USA 12345 (123) 456-7890	Worship Singers Joe Director 1234 Anystreet Anytown, USA 12345 (123) 456-7890

Prayer Ministry Director Joe Director 1234 Anystreet Anytown, USA 12345 (123) 456-7890		Prayer Ministry Asst. Dir. Joe Director 1234 Anystreet Anytown, USA 12345 (123) 456-7890
Early Morning Prayer Joe Director 1234 Anystreet Anytown, USA 12345 (123) 456-7890		Daily Prayer Joe Director 1234 Anystreet Anytown, USA 12345 (123) 456-7890
Monday Evening Prayer Joe Director 1234 Anystreet Anytown, USA 12345 (123) 456-7890	Wednesday Evening Prayer Joe Director 1234 Anystreet Anytown, USA 12345 (123) 456-7890	Friday Evening Prayer Joe Director 1234 Anystreet Anytown, USA 12345 (123) 456-7890

DISCIPLESHIP

Adult Sunday Bible School (AM) Joe Director 1234 Anystreet Anytown, USA 12345 (123) 456-7890	Adult Sunday Bible School (PM) John Director 1234 Anystreet Anytown, USA 12345 (123) 456-7890

Children's Sunday School (AM) Joe Director 1234 Anystreet Anytown, USA 12345 (123) 456-7890	Children's Sunday School (PM) John Director 1234 Anystreet Anytown, USA 12345 (123) 456-7890
Children's Church (AM) Joe Director 1234 Anystreet Anytown, USA 12345 (123) 456-7890	Children's Church (PM) John Director 1234 Anystreet Anytown, USA 12345 (123) 456-7890

Vision Bible Institute
1234 Anystreet
Anytown, USA 12345
(123) 456-7890

Wed. Sun. Baptism Class Joe Director 1234 Anystreet Anytown, USA 12345 (123) 456-7890	Wed. Discipleship Class John Director 1234 Anystreet Anytown, USA 12345 (123) 456-7890

FELLOWSHIP

Home Care Groups Joe Director 1234 Anystreet Anytown, USA 12345 (123) 456-7890	Women's Ministry Director Joe Director 1234 Anystreet Anytown, USA 12345 (123) 456-7890	Women's Ministry (AM) Joe Director 1234 Anystreet Anytown, USA 12345 (123) 456-7890
Women's Ministry (PM) Joe Director 1234 Anystreet Anytown, USA 12345 (123) 456-7890	Men's Ministry (AM) Joe Director 1234 Anystreet Anytown, USA 12345 (123) 456-7890	Men's Ministry (PM) Joe Director 1234 Anystreet Anytown, USA 12345 (123) 456-7890
Singles Ministry Director Joe Director 1234 Anystreet Anytown, USA 12345 (123) 456-7890	Singles Ministry Coordinator of Activities Joe Director 1234 Anystreet Anytown, USA 12345 (123) 456-7890	Youth Ministry Director Joe Director 1234 Anystreet Anytown, USA 12345 (123) 456-7890

SERVICE

Altar Workers Joe Director 1234 Anystreet Anytown, USA 12345 (123) 456-7890	**Evangelistic Teams** John Director 1234 Anystreet Anytown, USA 12345 (123) 456-7890
Hospitality Joe Director 1234 Anystreet Anytown, USA 12345 (123) 456-7890	**Mercy Missions** John Director 1234 Anystreet Anytown, USA 12345 (123) 456-7890
Nursery (AM) Joe Director 1234 Anystreet Anytown, USA 12345 (123) 456-7890	**Nursery (PM)** John Director 1234 Anystreet Anytown, USA 12345 (123) 456-7890
Senior Saints Ministry Joe Director 1234 Anystreet Anytown, USA 12345 (123) 456-7890	**Transportation** John Director 1234 Anystreet Anytown, USA 12345 (123) 456-7890
Ushers/Greeters (AM) Joe Director 1234 Anystreet Anytown, USA 12345 (123) 456-7890	**Ushers/Greeters (PM)** John Director 1234 Anystreet Anytown, USA 12345 (123) 456-7890

SERVICE

Communications Director Joe Director 1234 Anystreet Anytown, USA 12345 (123) 456-7890		
Audio Joe Director 1234 Anystreet Anytown, USA 12345 (123) 456-7890	Audio Joe Director 1234 Anystreet Anytown, USA 12345 (123) 456-7890	Audio Joe Director 1234 Anystreet Anytown, USA 12345 (123) 456-7890
Cassettes Joe Director 1234 Anystreet Anytown, USA 12345 (123) 456-7890	Radio Ministry Joe Director 1234 Anystreet Anytown, USA 12345 (123) 456-7890	

Vision Bookstore Joe Director 1234 Anystreet Anytown, USA 12345 (123) 456-7890		
Bookstore Assistant Joe Director 1234 Anystreet Anytown, USA 12345 (123) 456-7890	Bookstore Assistant Joe Director 1234 Anystreet Anytown, USA 12345 (123) 456-7890	Bookstore Assistant Joe Director 1234 Anystreet Anytown, USA 12345 (123) 456-7890

CHURCH STAFF

	Administrator Joe Director 1234 Anystreet Anytown, USA 12345 (123) 456-7890	
Secretary for Pastor & Administrator Joe Director 1234 Anystreet Anytown, USA 12345 (123) 456-7890	**Church Receptionist** Joe Director 1234 Anystreet Anytown, USA 12345 (123) 456-7890	**Accounts Payable** Joe Director 1234 Anystreet Anytown, USA 12345 (123) 456-7890
	Buildings Superintendent Joe Director 1234 Anystreet Anytown, USA 12345 (123) 456-7890	

VISION CHRISTIAN CENTER INTERNATIONAL CALENDAR OF EVENTS

Vision Christian Center International

Sunday	Monday	Tuesday	Wednesday	Thursday	Friday	Saturday
				1 New Year's Day Bldg. to Serve Emphasis 8:00 a.m. Elder/Deacon/ Ministers Fasting and Prayer	2	3 8:00 a.m. Lay Minister Prayer Breakfast
4 Prayer Week Children's Dedication	5 Prayer Week 7:30 p.m. VBI Winter Trimester Classes Begin	6 Prayer Week	7 Prayer Week	8 Prayer Week 7:30 p.m. VBI classes	9 Prayer Week 7:30 p.m. English VHS 7:30 p.m. Youth Service	10 Prayer Week 10:00 a.m. VCCI Teacher's Workshop
11 Lay Minister/Telecare Commissioning Service AM/PM	12	13 7:30 p.m. Deacons Meeting	14 7:30 p.m. Baptism Service	15	16 Young Adults Retreat 7:30 p.m. Board Meeting 7:30 p.m. Youth Service	17 Young Adults Retreat 9:00 a.m. Deacons/Ushers Breakfast
18 Missions Emphasis	19	20	21 7:30 p.m. Public Prayer Service	22	23 7:30 p.m. Spanish VHS 7:30 p.m. Youth Service	24
25 Commissioning Board of Elders/Deacons	26	27 7:30 p.m. Planning/Training Meeting – Nursery Workers 8:00 p.m. Staff Meeting	28	29	30 7:30 p.m. Youth Service	

January 2006 Sample

THE TEACHING MINISTRY OF DR. STAN DEKOVEN

Dr. Stan DeKoven conducts seminars and professional workshops, both nationally and internationally, based on his books and extensive experience in Practical Christian Living. He is available for limited engagements at Church Seminars, retreats and conferences. For a complete listing of topics, we invite you to contact:

DR. STAN DEKOVEN,
PRESIDENT VISION INTERNATIONAL UNIVERSITY
WALK IN WISDOM SEMINARS
RAMONA, CA 92065
(760) 789-4700 OR 1-800-9VISION
www.vienetwork.net/vision.edu/drstandekoven.com

OTHER HELPFUL BOOKS BY DR. DEKOVEN ON RELATED TOPICS INCLUDE:
Journey to Wholeness: Restoration of the Soul;
Marriage and Family Life: A Christian Perspective;
Grief Relief: Prescriptions for Pain after Significant Loss;
On Belay! Introduction to Christian Counseling;
Family Violence: Patterns of Destruction;
Forty Days to the Promise: A Way Through the Wilderness;
I Want To Be Like You, Dad: Breaking Free From Generational Patterns;
Visionary Leadership; A Study in Leadership Development
Christian Education: Principles and Practices;
Parenting on Purpose: A Practical Guide to Christian Parenting

www.ingramcontent.com/pod-product-compliance
Lightning Source LLC
Chambersburg PA
CBHW050815160426
43192CB00010B/1770